to

_____

from

100 DEVOTIONALS

GOD

really knowing Him

The quoted ideas expressed in this book (but not scripture verses) are not, in all cases, exact quotations, as some have been edited for clarity and brevity. In all cases, the author has attempted to maintain the speaker's original intent. In some cases, quoted material for this book was obtained from secondary sources, primarily print media. While every effort was made to ensure the accuracy of these sources, the accuracy cannot be guaranteed. For additions, deletions, corrections or clarifications in future editions of this text, please write FAMILY CHRISTIAN STORES.

Scripture quotations are taken from:

The Holy Bible, King James Version

The Holy Bible, New International Version (NIV) Copyright © 1973, 1978, 1984, by International Bible Society. Used by permission of Zondervan Publishing House. All rights reserved.

The New American Standard Bible®, (NASB) Copyright © 1960, 1962, 1963, 1968, 1971, 1972, 1973, 1975, 1977, 1995 by The Lockman Foundation. Used by permission.

The Holy Bible, New King James Version (NKJV) Copyright © 1982 by Thomas Nelson, Inc. Used by permission.

The Holy Bible, New Living Translation, (NLT) Copyright © 1996. Used by permission of Tyndale House Publishers, Inc., Wheaton, Illinois 60189. All rights reserved.

New Century Version®. (NCV) Copyright © 1987, 1988, 1991 by Word Publishing, a division of Thomas Nelson, Inc. All rights reserved. Used by permission.

The Holy Bible: Revised Standard Version (RSV). Copyright 1946, 1952, 1959, 1973 by the Division of Christian Education of the National Council of the Churches of Christ in the United States of America. All rights reserved. Used by permission.

The Holy Bible, The Living Bible (TLB), Copyright © 1971 owned by assignment by Illinois Regional Bank N.A. (as trustee). Used by permission of Tyndale House Publishers, Inc., Wheaton, Illinois 60189. All rights reserved.

The Message (MSG) This edition issued by contractual arrangement with NavPress, a division of The Navigators, U.S.A. Originally published by NavPress in English as THE MESSAGE: The Bible in Contemporary Language copyright 2002-2003 by Eugene Peterson. All rights reserved.

The Holman Christian Standard Bible™ (Holman CSB) Copyright © 1999, 2000, 2001 by Holman Bible Publishers. Used by permission.

Cover Design by Kim Russell / Wahoo Designs

Page Layout by Bart Dawson

ISBN 1-58334-359-8

ISBN-13 978-1-58334-359-3

Printed in the United States of America

100 DEVOTIONALS

GOD

Introduction

Can you spare two minutes each day for God? Of course you can . . . and of course you should! Scottish-born evangelist Henry Drummond correctly observed, "Ten minutes spent in Christ's company every day—even two minutes—will make the whole day different." How true. If you dedicate even a few minutes each morning to devotional reading and prayer, you will change the tone and direction of your life.

This text contains 100 quick devotionals that are intended to help you gain a better understanding of your Heavenly Father and His only begotten Son. Each chapter contains Biblically-based principles for building your faith and your life. So, during the next 100 days, read a chapter each day and take each day's message to heart. Hopefully, by the time you get to the end of the book, you'll have a better understanding—and a greater appreciation—for your unfolding relationship with God.

Are you willing to allow God to work in you and through you? Are you willing to establish a life-altering relationship with your Creator? And do you desire the eternal abundance and peace that can be yours through God's Son? If so, ask for God's guidance many times each day . . . starting with a regular daily devotional. When you do, you will soon discover that your Heavenly Father is not just near, He is here. And He is always ready to transform you into a new creation if and when you really get to know Him.

He's Right Here, Right Now

The LORD is with you when you are with Him.
If you seek Him, He will be found by you.

2 CHRONICLES 15:2 HOLMAN CSB

Do you ever wonder if God is really "right here, right now"? Do you wonder if God hears your prayers, if He understands your feelings, or if He really knows your heart? If so, you're not alone: lots of very faithful Christians have experienced periods of doubt. In fact, some of the biggest heroes in the Bible had plenty of doubts—and so, perhaps, will you. But when you have doubts, remember this: God isn't on a coffee break, and He hasn't moved out of town. God isn't taking a long vacation, and He isn't snoozing on the couch. He's right here, right now, listening to your thoughts and prayers, watching over your every move.

If you'd like to get to know God a little bit better, He's always available—always ready to listen to your prayers and always ready to speak to your heart. Are you ready to talk to Him? If so, congratulations. If not, what are you waiting for?

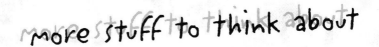

The tender eyes of God perpetually see us.
He has never stopped noticing.

ANGELA THOMAS

God expresses His love toward us by His uninterrupted
presence in our lives.

CHARLES STANLEY

God's presence is with you, but you have to make
a choice to believe—and I mean, really believe—
that this is true. This conscious decision is yours alone.

BILL HYBELS

The Big Idea

If God is everywhere, why does He sometimes seem so
distant? That's a question that has less to do with God and
more to do with us. When God seems far away, it's because
we have allowed ourselves to become distant from Him, not
vice versa.

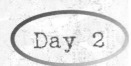

Get to Know His Son

Then Jesus spoke to them again, saying,
"I am the light of the world. He who follows Me shall not
walk in darkness, but have the light of life."
John 8:12 NKJV

There's really no way around it: If you want to know God, you've got to get to know His Son. And that's good, because getting to know Jesus can—and should—be the most enriching experience of your life.

Can you honestly say that you're passionate about your faith and that you're really following Jesus? Hopefully so. But if you're preoccupied with other things—or if you're strictly a one-day-a-week Christian—then you're in need of a major-league spiritual makeover.

Jesus doesn't want you to be a lukewarm believer; Jesus wants you to be a "new creation" through Him. And that's exactly what you should want for yourself, too. Nothing is more important than your wholehearted commitment to your Creator and to His only begotten Son. Your faith must never be an afterthought; it must be your ultimate priority, your ultimate possession, and your ultimate passion.

more stuff to think about

Our responsibility is to feed from Him, to stay close to Him,
to follow Him—because sheep easily go astray—
so that we eternally experience the protection and
companionship of our Great Shepherd the Lord Jesus Christ.

FRANKLIN GRAHAM

Think of this—we may live together with Him here and now,
a daily walking with Him who loved us
and gave Himself for us.

ELISABETH ELLIOT

To walk out of His will is to walk into nowhere.

C. S. LEWIS

The Big Idea

When Jesus endured His sacrifice on the cross, He paid a
terrible price for you. What price are you willing to pay for
Him?

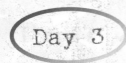
If You Reach Out
to God . . .

Draw near to God, and He will draw near to you.
JAMES 4:8 HOLMAN CSB

Okay, God has made a very important promise to you: He's promised that if you try to find Him, He won't hide. In fact, the opposite is true: if you sincerely try to know Him better, He'll help.

How, exactly, can you learn more about God . . . and how can you grow closer to Him? By Bible study, prayer, worship, praise, and a time of regular daily devotion, for starters. You should also associate with like-minded believers, and you should listen carefully to the small, quiet voice that God has placed within your heart. Finally, you should form a life-altering, soul-transforming relationship with God's only begotten Son. When you do these things, you'll open yourself to the Creator, and you'll be forever glad that you did. Forever.

2 minutes A DAY

more stuff to think about

Slowly and surely, we learn the great secret of life,
which is to know God.

OSWALD CHAMBERS

God does the finding, and our seeking is,
even from the first movement within our souls,
an active response to his finding us.

R. PAUL STEVENS

There is nothing on earth that can satisfy
our deepest longing. We long to see God.
The leaves of life are rustling with the rumor that we will—
and we won't be satisfied until we do.

MAX LUCADO

The Big Idea

Nobody can find Him for you. God is searching for you;
it's up to you—and you alone—to open your heart to Him.

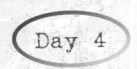

Pray

*Be cheerful no matter what; pray all the time;
thank God no matter what happens. This is the way God
wants you who belong to Christ Jesus to live.*

1 Thessalonians 5:16-18 MSG

If you genuinely desire to know God, then you must pray . . . a lot.

Is prayer an integral part of your daily life, or is it a hit-or-miss habit? Do you "pray without ceasing," or is your prayer life an afterthought? Do you regularly pray in the quiet moments of the early morning, or do you bow your head only when others are watching? If your prayers have become more a matter of habit than a matter of passion, you're robbing yourself of a deeper relationship with God. And how can you rectify this situation? By praying more frequently and more fervently. God is always near, and He's always ready to hear from you. So don't worry about things; pray about them. God is waiting . . . and listening!

more stuff to think about

If in everything you seek Jesus, you will doubtless find him.
But if you seek yourself, you will indeed find yourself,
to your own ruin. For you do yourself more harm by
not seeking Jesus than the whole world
and all your enemies could do to you.

THOMAS À KEMPIS

I approach prayer in a similar way as I experience
the joy of relationship with God. No matter how severe
"the winter of the soul" may have been, standing
in the presence of God brings pure joy.

HENRY BLACKABY

The Big Idea

Eyelids closed . . . or not! When you are praying, the
position of your eyelids makes little or no difference. Of
course it's good to close your eyes and bow your head
whenever you can, but it's also good to offer quick prayers
to God with your eyes—and your heart—wide open.

Meet with God Every Morning

Morning by morning he wakens me and opens my understanding to his will. The Sovereign LORD has spoken to me, and I have listened.

ISAIAH 50:4-5 NLT

Want to know God better? Then schedule a meeting with Him every day.

Daily life is a tapestry of habits, and no habit is more important to your spiritual health than the discipline of daily prayer and devotion to the Creator. When you begin each day with your head bowed and your heart lifted, you are reminded of God's love and God's laws.

When you do engage in a regular regimen of worship and praise, God will reward you for your wisdom and your obedience. Each new day is a gift from God, and if you're wise, you'll spend a few quiet moments thanking the Giver. It's a wonderful way to start your day.

2 Minutes A Day

more stuff to think about

A person with no devotional life generally struggles
with faith and obedience.

CHARLES STANLEY

Maintenance of the devotional mood is indispensable to
success in the Christian life.

A. W. TOZER

Mark it down. God never turns away the honest seeker.
Go to God with your questions. You may not find
all the answers, but in finding God,
you know the One who does.

MAX LUCADO

The Big Idea

Get reacquainted with God every day: Would you like a
foolproof formula for a better relationship with your Creator?
Then stay in close contact with Him.

Praise Him!

I will praise You with my whole heart.

PSALM 138:1 NKJV

I f you're like most folks on the planet, you're a very busy person. Your life is probably hectic, demanding, and complicated. And when the demands of life leave you rushing from place to place with scarcely a moment to spare, you may not take time to praise your Creator. Big mistake.

The Bible makes it clear: it pays to praise God. Worship and praise should be a part of everything you do. Otherwise, you quickly lose perspective as you fall prey to the demands of everyday life.

Do you sincerely desire to know God in a more meaningful way? Then praise Him for who He is and for what He has done for you. And please don't wait until Sunday morning—praise Him all day long, every day, for as long as you live . . . and then for all eternity.

more stuff to think about

Praise opens the window of our hearts, preparing us to walk
more closely with God. Prayer raises the window of our
spirit, enabling us to listen more clearly to the Father.

MAX LUCADO

Praising God is one of the highest and
purest acts of religion. In prayer we act like men;
in praise we act like angels.

THOMAS WATSON

Most of the verses written about praise in God's Word were
voiced by people faced with crushing heartaches, injustice,
treachery, slander, and scores of other difficult situations.

JONI EARECKSON TADA

The Big Idea

Praise Him! One of the big reasons you should attend
church is to praise God. But, you need not wait until Sunday
rolls around to thank your Heavenly Father. Instead, you can
praise Him many times each day by saying silent prayers that
only He can hear.

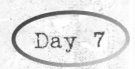

Day 7

Experience the Joy

Always be full of joy in the Lord. I say it again—rejoice!
PHILIPPIANS 4:4 NLT

You can't really get to know God until you genuinely experience God's joy for yourself. It's not enough to hear somebody else talk about being a joyful Christian—you must experience Christ's joy in order to understand it. Does that mean that you'll be a joy-filled believer 24 hours a day, seven days a week, from this moment on? Nope. But it does mean that you can experience God's joy personally, frequently, and intensely.

So, here's a prescription for better spiritual health: Open the door of your soul to Christ. When you do, He will give you peace and joy . . . heaping helpings of peace and joy.

2 minutes a day

more stuff to think about

Rejoice, the Lord is King; Your Lord and King adore!
Rejoice, give thanks and sing and triumph evermore.

CHARLES WESLEY

Every morning is a fresh opportunity to find
God's extraordinary joy in the most ordinary places.

JANET. L. WEAVER

We all go through pain and sorrow, but the presence of
God, like a warm, comforting blanket, can shield us and
protect us, and allow the deep inner joy to surface,
even in the most devastating circumstances.

BARBARA JOHNSON

The Big Idea

Joy begins with a choice: the choice to establish a genuine
relationship with God and His Son. As Amy Carmichael
correctly observed, "Joy is not gush; joy is not mere jolliness.
Joy is perfect acquiescence, acceptance, and rest in God's
will, whatever comes."

Get Involved in a Church

For we are God's fellow workers; you are God's field, you are God's building.

1 CORINTHIANS 3:9 NKJV

One way that we come to know God is by involving ourselves in His church.

In the book of Acts, Luke reminds us to "feed the church of God" (20:28). As Christians who have been saved by a loving, compassionate Creator, we are compelled not only to worship Him in our hearts but also to worship Him in the presence of fellow believers.

Do you attend church regularly? And when you attend, are you an active participant, or are you just taking up space? The answer to these questions will have a profound impact on the quality and direction of your spiritual journey.

So do yourself a favor: become actively involved in your church. Don't just go to church out of habit. Go to church out of a sincere desire to know and worship God. When you do, you'll be blessed by the One who sent His Son to die so that you might have everlasting life.

2 MINUTES A DAY

more stuff to think about

The Bible knows nothing of solitary religion.

JOHN WESLEY

The church needs the power and the gifts of
the Holy Spirit more now than ever before.

CORRIE TEN BOOM

It has always been the work of the church to
bring others to belief in Christ and to experience
a personal relationship with Him.

CHARLES STANLEY

The Big Idea

Make church a celebration, not an obligation: Your attitude
towards church is important, in part, because it is contagious
. . . so celebrate accordingly!

The Right Kind of Fellowship

So reach out and welcome one another to God's glory.
Jesus did it; now you do it!
ROMANS 15:7 MSG

If you genuinely want to build a closer relationship with God, you need to build closer relationships with godly people. That's why fellowship with likeminded believers should be an integral part of your life. Your association with fellow Christians should be uplifting, enlightening, encouraging, and (above all) consistent.

Are your friends the kind of people who encourage you to seek God's will and to obey God's Word? If so, you've chosen your friends wisely. And that's a good thing because when you choose friends who honor God, you'll find it easier to honor Him, too.

2 minutes A DAY

more stuff to think about

Brotherly love is still the distinguishing badge
of every true Christian.

MATTHEW HENRY

Real fellowship happens when people get honest about
who they are and what is happening in their lives.

RICK WARREN

I hope you will find a few folks who walk with God to also
walk with you through the seasons of your life.

JOHN ELDREDGE

The Big Idea

Christians are not Lone Rangers. They are members of a
spiritual family, and they need one another.

Ask Him

*And yet the reason you don't have what you want
is that you don't ask God for it.*
JAMES 4:2 NLT

If you want to know more about God, ask for His help!
When you ask sincerely—and repeatedly—He will answer
your request.

How often do you ask God for His guidance and
His wisdom? Occasionally? Intermittently? Whenever
you experience a crisis? Hopefully not. Hopefully, you've
acquired the habit of asking for God's assistance early and
often. And hopefully, you have learned to seek His guidance
in every aspect of your life.

Do you sincerely seek to know God's unfolding plans
for you? If so, ask Him for direction, for protection, and for
strength—and then keep asking Him every day that you live.
Whatever your need, no matter how great or small, pray
about it and have faith. God is not just near; He is here, and
He's perfectly capable of answering your prayers. Now, it's
up to you to ask.

more stuff to think about

We honor God by asking for great things when
they are a part of His promise. We dishonor Him
and cheat ourselves when we ask for molehills
where He has promised mountains.

VANCE HAVNER

Notice that we must ask. And we will sometimes
struggle to hear and struggle with what we hear.
But personally, it's worth it. I'm after the path of life—
and he alone knows it.

JOHN ELDREDGE

We get into trouble when we think we know what to do
and we stop asking God if we're doing it.

STORMIE OMARTIAN

The Big Idea

Ask Him, and then be patient. Remember, God answers
prayers based on His timetable, not yours.

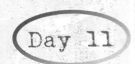

Day 11

Bitterness Puts Distance Between You and God

Hatred stirs up trouble, but love forgives all wrongs.
PROVERBS 10:12 NCV

If you're unwilling to forgive other people, you're building a roadblock between yourself and God. And the less you're willing to forgive, the bigger your roadblock. So if you want to know God in a more meaningful way, you must learn how to forgive and, to the best of your abilities, forget.

Is there someone out there you need to forgive? If so, pray for that person. And then pray for yourself by asking God to heal your heart. Don't expect forgiveness to be easy or quick, but rest assured: with God as your partner, you can forgive . . . and you will.

2 MINUTES A DAY

more stuff to think about

He who cannot forgive others breaks the bridge over
which he himself must pass.

CORRIE TEN BOOM

Bitterness is a spiritual cancer, a rapidly growing malignancy
that can consume your life. Bitterness cannot be ignored
but must be healed at the very core,
and only Christ can heal bitterness.

BETH MOORE

Forgiveness enables you to bury your grudge in icy earth.
To put the past behind you. To flush resentment away by
being the first to forgive. Forgiveness fashions your future.
It is a brave and brash thing to do.

BARBARA JOHNSON

The Big Idea

Holding a grudge? Drop it! Remember, holding a grudge is
like letting somebody live rent-free in your brain . . . so don't
do it!

Be Still

Be still, and know that I am God.
PSALM 46:10 NKJV

The Bible teaches that a wonderful way to get to know God is simply to be still and listen to Him. But sometimes, you may find it hard to slow down and listen. As the demands of everyday life weigh down upon you, you may be tempted to ignore God's presence or—worse yet—to rebel against His commandments. But, when you quiet yourself and acknowledge His presence, God touches your heart and restores your spirits. So why not let Him do it right now? If you really want to know Him better, silence is a wonderful place to start.

more stuff to think about

Be still: pause and discover that God is God.

CHARLES SWINDOLL

I have come to recognize that He never asks us to do
anything He has not already done. He never takes us
anyplace where He has not been ahead of us.
What He is after is not performance,
but a relationship with us.

GLORIA GAITHER

I always begin my prayers in silence,
for it is in the silence of the heart that God speaks.

MOTHER TERESA

The Big Idea

Want to talk to God? Then don't make Him shout.
If you really want to hear from God, go to a quiet place
and listen. If you keep listening long enough and carefully
enough, He'll start talking.

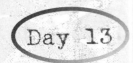

Serve Him

*So prepare your minds for service and have self-control.
All your hope should be for the gift of grace that will be
yours when Jesus Christ is shown to you.*

1 Peter 1:13 NCV

The words of Jesus are clear: the most esteemed men and women in this world are not the big-shots who jump up on stage and hog the spotlight; the greatest among us are those who are willing to become humble servants.

Are you willing to become a servant for Christ? Are you willing to pitch in and make the world a better place, or are you determined to keep all your blessings to yourself? Hopefully, you are determined to follow Christ's example by making yourself an unselfish servant to those who need your help.

If you seek to walk with the One from Galilee, you must become an unselfish servant. In truth, there's simply no other way to follow Jesus.

more stuff to think about

Christianity, in its purest form, is nothing more than seeing Jesus. Christian service, in its purest form, is nothing more than imitating him who we see. To see his Majesty and to imitate him: that is the sum of Christianity.

MAX LUCADO

In God's family, there is to be one great body of people: servants. In fact, that's the way to the top in his kingdom.

CHARLES SWINDOLL

A wholehearted love for God looks to Him through His Word and prayer, always watching and waiting, ever ready to do all that He says, prepared to act on His expressed desires.

ELIZABETH GEORGE

The Big Idea

Jesus was a servant, and if you want to follow Him, you must be a servant, too—even when service requires sacrifice.

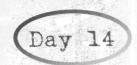

Do the Right Thing

Blessed are those who hunger and thirst for righteousness,
for they will be filled.
MATTHEW 5:6 NIV

If you want to know God, you should obey God. But obeying Him isn't always easy. You live in a world that presents countless temptations to stray far from God's path. So, here's some timely advice: when you're confronted with sin, walk—or better yet run—in the opposite direction.

When you seek righteousness for yourself—and when we seek the companionship of people who do likewise—you will reap the spiritual rewards that God has in store for you. When you live in accordance with God's commandments, you will be blessed. When you genuinely seek to follow in the footsteps of God's Son, you will experience God's presence, God's peace, and God's abundance.

So, make yourself this promise: Support only those activities that further God's kingdom and your own spiritual growth. Then, prepare to reap the blessings that God has promised to all those who live according to His will and His Word.

more stuff to think about

Our souls were made to live in an upper atmosphere,
and we stifle and choke if we live on any lower level.
Our eyes were made to look off from these heavenly heights,
and our vision is distorted by any lower gazing.

HANNAH WHITALL SMITH

Come work for the Lord. The work is hard,
the hours are long, and the pay is low,
but the retirement benefits are out of this world.

ANONYMOUS

Righteousness not only defines God,
but God defines righteousness.

BILL HYBELS

The Big Idea

If you're not sure that it's the right thing to do . . . slow down
and listen to your conscience. Remember this: God gave you
a conscience for one reason—to use it.

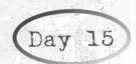

Give God Your Complete Attention

Worship the Lord your God and . . . serve Him only.

MATTHEW 4:10 HOLMAN CSB

Who rules your heart? Is it God, or is it something else? Do you give God your firstfruits or your last? Have you given Christ your heart, your soul, your talents, your time, and your testimony, or have you given Him little more than a few hours each Sunday morning?

In the book of Exodus, God warns that we should place no gods before Him. Yet all too often, we place our Lord in second, third, or fourth place as we worship the gods of pride, greed, power, or lust. When we unwittingly place possessions or relationships above our love for the Creator, we must seek His forgiveness and repent from our sins.

Does God rule your heart? Make certain that the honest answer to this question is a resounding yes. In the life of every righteous believer, God comes first. And that's precisely the place that He deserves in your heart.

more stuff to think about

God is everything. My focus must be on him,
seeking to know him more completely
and allowing him full possession of my life.

MARY MORRISON SUGGS

I have so much to do that I shall spend
the first three hours of the day in prayer.

MARTIN LUTHER

The greatest enemy of holiness is not passion; it is apathy.

JOHN ELDREDGE

The Big Idea

The world wants you to pay attention to its distractions and
temptations. God wants you to pay attention to His Son.
Trust God.

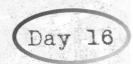

Date People Who Know God

Do you think I am trying to make people accept me?
No, God is the One I am trying to please.
Am I trying to please people? If I still wanted to please
people, I would not be a servant of Christ.

GALATIANS 1:10 NCV

Is God a part of your dating life? Hopefully so. If you sincerely want to know God, then you should date people who feel the same way.

If you're still searching for Mr. or Mrs. Right (while trying to avoid falling in love with Mr. or Mrs. Wrong), be patient, be prudent, and be picky. Look for someone whose values you respect, whose behavior you approve of, and whose faith you admire. Remember that appearances can be deceiving and tempting, so watch your step. And when it comes to the important task of building a lifetime relationship with the guy or girl of your dreams, pray about it!

When it comes to your dating life, God wants to give His approval—or not—but He won't give it until He's asked. So ask, listen, and decide accordingly.

more stuff to think about

We discover our role in life through
our relationships with others.

RICK WARREN

It wasn't the apple, it was the pair.

ANONYMOUS

Make God's will the focus of your life day by day.
If you seek to please Him and Him alone,
you'll find yourself satisfied with life.

KAY ARTHUR

The Big Idea

Place God first in every aspect of your life, including your
dating life: He deserves first place, and any relationship that
doesn't put Him there is the wrong relationship for you.

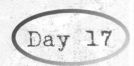

Look for Miracles

*God verified the message by signs and wonders
and various miracles and by giving gifts of the Holy Spirit
whenever he chose to do so.*

HEBREWS 2:4 NLT

One way to know more about God is to look carefully at the miraculous things that He does. But sometimes, we're simply too preoccupied to notice. Instead of paying careful attention to God's handiwork, we become distracted. Instead of expecting God to work miracles, we become cynical. Instead of depending on God's awesome power, we seek to muddle along using our own power—with decidedly mixed results.

Miracles, both great and small, are an integral part of everyday life—and they are a part of your life, too. But here's the million-dollar question: have you noticed?

If you lack the faith that God can work miracles in your own life, it's time to reconsider. Instead of doubting God, trust His power, and expect His miracles. Then, wait patiently . . . because something miraculous is about to happen.

2 minutes A DAY

more stuff to think about

When God is involved, anything can happen.
Be open and stay that way. God has a beautiful way of
bringing good vibrations out of broken chords.

CHARLES SWINDOLL

The healing acts of Jesus were themselves a message
that he had come to set men free.

FRANCIS MACNUTT

I could go through this day oblivious to the miracles
all around me or I could tune in and "enjoy."

GLORIA GAITHER

The Big Idea

If you're looking for miracles . . . you'll find them. If you're
not, you won't.

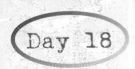

Overcome Pessimism

Give your worries to the Lord, and he will take care of you.
He will never let good people down.
PSALM 55:22 NCV

Pessimism and Christianity don't mix. Why? Because Christians have every reason to be optimistic about life here on earth and life eternal. As C. H. Spurgeon observed, "Our hope in Christ for the future is the mainstream of our joy." But sometimes, we fall prey to worry, frustration, anxiety, or sheer exhaustion, and our hearts become heavy. What's needed is plenty of rest, a large dose of perspective, and God's healing touch, but not necessarily in that order.

Today, make this promise to yourself and keep it: vow to be a hope-filled Christian. Think optimistically about your life and your future. Trust your hopes, not your fears. Take time to celebrate God's glorious creation. And then, when you've filled your heart with hope and gladness, share your optimism with others. They'll be better for it, and so will you. But not necessarily in that order.

more stuff to think about

To lose heart is to lose everything.

JOHN ELDREDGE

A pessimist is someone who believes that when her cup runneth over she'll need a mop.

BARBARA JOHNSON

Never yield to gloomy anticipation. Place your hope and confidence in God. He has no record of failure.

MRS. CHARLES E. COWMAN

The Big Idea

If you genuinely believe that God is good and that His Son died for your sins, how can you be pessimistic about your future? The answer, of course, is that you can't!

Don't Get Too Attached to the World

Don't love the world's ways. Don't love the world's goods. Love of the world squeezes out love for the Father. Practically everything that goes on in the world—wanting your own way, wanting everything for yourself, wanting to appear important—has nothing to do with the Father. It just isolates you from him. The world and all its wanting, wanting, wanting is on the way out—but whoever does what God wants is set for eternity.

1 John 2:15-17 MSG

Our world is filled with pressures: some good, some bad. The pressures that we feel to follow God's will and obey His commandments are positive pressures. God places them on our hearts so that we might act in accordance with His will. But we also face different pressures, ones that are definitely not from God. When we feel pressured to do things—or even to think thoughts—that lead us away from Him, we must beware.

Many elements of society seek to mold us into more worldly beings; God, on the other hand, seeks to mold us into new beings, new creations through Christ, beings that are most certainly not conformed to this world. If we are to

2 MINUTES A DAY

please God, we must resist the pressures that society seeks to impose upon us, and we must conform ourselves, instead, to His will, to His path, and to His Son.

more stuff to think about

The socially prescribed affluent, middle-class lifestyle has become so normative in our churches that we discern little conflict between it and the Christian lifestyle prescribed in the New Testament.

TONY CAMPOLO

He who dies with the most toys . . . still dies.

ANONYMOUS

The more we stuff ourselves with material pleasures, the less we seem to appreciate life.

BARBARA JOHNSON

The Big Idea

Getting a little greedy? Pray without seizing.

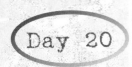

Don't Give Up on God or Yourself

Thanks be to God! He gives us the victory through our Lord Jesus Christ. Therefore, my dear brothers, stand firm. Let nothing move you. Always give yourselves fully to the work of the Lord, because you know that your labor in the Lord is not in vain.

1 CORINTHIANS 15:57-58 NIV

Do you sincerely want to know God and live a life that is pleasing to Him? If so, you must remember that life is not a sprint, it's a marathon that calls for preparation, determination, and lots of perseverance.

Are you one of those people who doesn't give up easily, or are you quick to bail out when the going gets tough? If you've developed the unfortunate habit of giving up at the first sign of trouble, it's probably time for you to have a heart-to-heart talk with the person you see every time you look in the mirror.

Jesus finished what He began, and so should you. Despite His suffering, despite the shame of the cross, Jesus was steadfast in His faithfulness to God. You, too, must remain faithful, especially when times are tough.

2 MINUTES A DAY

Do you want to build a closer relationship with God? Then don't give up. And if you're facing a difficult situation, remember this: whatever your problem, God can handle it. Your job is to keep persevering until He does.

more stuff to think about

God never gives up on you,
so don't you ever give up on Him.

MARIE T. FREEMAN

Only the man who follows the command of Jesus single-mindedly and unresistingly lets his yoke rest upon him, finds his burden easy, and under its gentle pressure receives the power to persevere in the right way.

DIETRICH BONHOEFFER

The Big Idea

If things don't work out at first, don't quit. If you never try, you'll never know how good you can be.

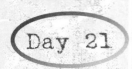

Study God's Word

*Every part of Scripture is God-breathed and useful one
way or another, showing us truth, exposing our rebellion,
correcting our mistakes, training us to live God's way.
Through the Word we are put together and
shaped up for the tasks God has for us.*

2 TIMOTHY 3:16-17 MSG

If you want to know God, you should read the book He
wrote. It's called the Bible, and it is one of the most
important tools that God uses to direct your steps and
transform your life.

As you seek to build a deeper relationship with your
Creator, you must decide whether God's Word will be a
bright spotlight that guides your path every day or a tiny
nightlight that occasionally flickers in the dark. The decision
to study the Bible—or not—is yours and yours alone. But
make no mistake: the way that you choose to use your Bible
will have a profound impact on you and your loved ones.

more stuff to think about

Walking in faith brings you to the Word of God.
There you will be healed, cleansed, fed, nurtured,
equipped, and matured.

KAY ARTHUR

I suggest you discipline yourself to spend time daily in
a systematic reading of God's Word.
Make this "quiet time" a priority that nobody can change.

WARREN WIERSBE

The Big Idea

Wisdom 101: If you're looking for wisdom, the book of
Proverbs is a wonderful place to start. It has 31 chapters,
one for each day of the month. If you read Proverbs
regularly, and if you take its teachings to heart, you'll gain
timeless wisdom from God's unchanging Word.

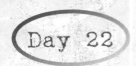

Don't Fall for Media Hype

*Don't copy the behavior and customs of this world,
but let God transform you into a new person by changing
the way you think. Then you will know what God wants you
to do, and you will know how good and pleasing
and perfect his will really is.*

ROMANS 12:2 NLT

The media is working around the clock in an attempt to rearrange your priorities. The media says that your appearance is all-important, that your clothes are all-important, that your car is all-important, and that partying is all-important. But guess what? Those messages are lies. The important things in your life have little to do with parties or appearances. The all-important things in life have to do with your faith, your family, and your future. Period.

So, here's a question for you: will you focus on God's messages or the media's messages? The answer should be obvious.

2 minutes A DAY

more stuff to think about

It's sobering to contemplate how much time, effort, sacrifice, compromise, and attention we give to acquiring and increasing our supply of something that is totally insignificant in eternity.

ANNE GRAHAM LOTZ

Nothing is more foolish than a security built upon the world and its promises, for they are all vanity and a lie.

MATTHEW HENRY

The Big Idea

Talk to your friends about the messages that you receive from the popular media, and compare those messages to the teachings of God's Word. Discuss ways that you can protect yourself and your family from the temptations and distractions of everyday life here in the 21st-century. And while you're at it, ask yourself this question: Does God really approve of every single TV show (and movie) that I watch?

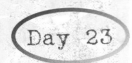
Day 23

Want Spiritual Growth? Pray!

Don't burn out; keep yourselves fueled and aflame.
Be alert servants of the Master, cheerfully expectant.
Don't quit in hard times; pray all the harder.
<small>ROMANS 12:11-12 MSG</small>

The quality of your spiritual life will be in direct proportion to the quality of your prayer life: the more you pray, the closer you will feel to God. So today, instead of turning things over in your mind, turn them over to God in prayer. Don't limit your prayers to the dinner table or the bedside table. Pray constantly about things great and small, and ask God to lead you to a place of His choosing. your Heavenly Father is always listening . . . and the rest is up to you.

2 minutes A DAY

more stuff to think about

The more a man bows his knee before God,
the straighter he stands before men.

ANONYMOUS

Whatever may be our circumstances in life,
may each one of us really believe that by way of
the Throne we have unlimited power.

ANNIE ARMSTRONG

I have acted like I'm all alone, but the truth is that
I never will be. When my prayers are weak, God is listening.
When my words are rote, God is listening.
When my heart is dry, amazingly God is still listening.

ANGELA THOMAS

The Big Idea

Prayer strengthens your relationship with God . . . so pray.
Martin Luther observed, "If I should neglect prayer but a
single day, I should lose a great deal of the fire of faith."
Those words apply to you, too. And it's up to you to live—
and to pray—accordingly.

Learn to Trust God

Lord, I give myself to you; my God, I trust you.
PSALM 25:1-2 NCV

If you want to know God, then you must learn to trust God. Yet, sometimes, when you feel overwhelmed by fears and doubts, you'll find that trusting God is difficult. So, here's a question for you to ponder: Are you willing to trust God completely, or are you still sitting squarely on the spiritual fence? The answer to this question will determine the tone, the quality, and the direction of your life.

Trusting God means trusting Him with every aspect of your life. You must trust Him with your relationships, your dreams, your finances, and your career. You must follow His commandments, and you must pray for His guidance.

When you trust your Heavenly Father without reservation, you can be sure that, in His own fashion and in His own time, God will reveal Himself to you in ways that you never could have imagined. So trust Him. And then prepare yourself for the abundance and the joy that will most certainly be yours when you do.

more stuff to think about

Even more than we long to be heard, God desires to listen.

ANGELA THOMAS

As God's children, we are the recipients of lavish love—
a love that motivates us to keep trusting
even when we have no idea what God is doing.

BETH MOORE

It helps to resign as the controller of your fate.
All that energy we expend to keep things running right
is not what keeps things running right.

ANNE LAMOTT

The Big Idea

It's simple: depend upon God. And while you're at it,
remember the words of Vance Havner: "We must live in
all kinds of days, both high days and low days, in simple
dependence upon Christ as the branch on the vine. This is
the supreme experience."

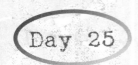

Day 25

Worship Every Day

Worship the Lord your God and . . . serve Him only.
MATTHEW 4:10 HOLMAN CSB

If you really want to know God, you must be willing to worship Him seven days a week, not just on Sunday. God has a wonderful plan for your life, and an important part of that plan includes the time that you set aside for praise and worship. Every life, including yours, is based upon some form of worship. The question is not whether you will worship, but what you worship.

If you choose to worship God, you will receive a bountiful harvest of joy, peace, and abundance. But if you distance yourself from God by foolishly worshiping earthly possessions and personal gratification, you're making a huge mistake. So do this: Worship God today and every day. Worship Him with sincerity and thanksgiving. Write His name on your heart and rest assured that He, too, has written your name on His.

2 minutes A DAY

more stuff to think about

Worship is wonder, love, and praise. Not only does it
cause us to contemplate and appreciate our holy God,
but it gives us vitality, vigor, and a desire to obey Him.

FRANKLIN GRAHAM

Worship is a voluntary act of gratitude offered
by the saved to the Savior, by the healed to the Healer,
by the delivered to the Deliverer.

MAX LUCADO

The Big Idea

Worship is not meant to be boxed up in a church building
on Sunday morning. To the contrary, praise and worship
should be woven into the very fabric of your life. Do you take
time each day to worship your Father in heaven, or do you
wait until Sunday morning to praise Him for His blessings?
The answer to this question will, in large part, determine the
quality and direction of your life. So worship accordingly.

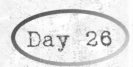

Choose Wise Role Models

A wise man will hear and increase learning,
and a man of understanding will attain wise counsel.
PROVERBS 1:5 NKJV

ere's a simple yet effective way to strengthen your faith: Choose role models whose faith in God is strong.

When you emulate godly people, you become a more godly person yourself. That's why you should seek out mentors who, by their words and their presence, make you a better person and a better Christian.

Today, as a gift to yourself, select, from your friends and family members, a mentor whose judgement you trust. Then listen carefully to your mentor's advice and be willing to accept that advice, even if accepting it requires effort or pain, or both. Consider your mentor to be God's gift to you. Thank God for that gift, and use it for the glory of His kingdom.

more stuff to think about

The effective mentor strives to help a man or woman discover what they can be in Christ and then holds them accountable to become that person.

HOWARD HENDRICKS

God often keeps us on the path by guiding us through the counsel of friends and trusted spiritual advisors.

BILL HYBELS

It takes a wise person to give good advice, but an even wiser person to take it.

MARIE T. FREEMAN

The Big Idea

Need advice? Talk to the experts. Your mentors may not have all of the answers, but at least they'll know most of the questions! So ask, listen, and learn.

Too Busy?

Be careful not to forget the LORD.
DEUTERONOMY 6:12 HOLMAN CSB

Each day has 1,440 minutes—do you value your relationship with God enough to spend a few of those minutes with Him? He deserves that much of your time and more. But if you find that you're simply "too busy" for a daily chat with your Father in heaven, it's time to take a long, hard look at your priorities and your values.

If you've acquired the unfortunate habit of trying to "squeeze" God into the corners of your life, it's time to reshuffle the items on your to-do list by placing God first. God wants your undivided attention, not the leftovers of your day. So, if you haven't already done so, form the habit of spending quality time with your Creator. He deserves it . . . and so, for that matter, do you.

more stuff to think about

Christ is not valued at all unless He is valued above all.

ST. AUGUSTINE

The prayer of the feeblest saint who lives in the Spirit and keeps right with God is terror to Satan. The very powers of darkness are paralyzed by prayer. It is no wonder that Satan tries to keep our minds fussy in active work till we cannot think in prayer.

OSWALD CHAMBERS

Often our lives are strangled by things that don't ultimatley matter.

GRADY NUTT

The Big Idea

Do first things first, and keep your focus on high-priority tasks. And remember this: your highest priority should be your relationship with God and His Son.

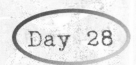

Put Faith Above Feelings

Now the just shall live by faith.
HEBREWS 10:38 NKJV

Hebrews 10:38 teaches that we should live by faith. Yet, sometimes, despite our best intentions, negative feelings can rob us of the peace and abundance that would otherwise be ours through Christ. When anger or anxiety separates us from the spiritual blessings that God has in store, we must rethink our priorities and renew our faith. And we must place faith above feelings. Human emotions are highly variable, decidedly unpredictable, and often unreliable. Our emotions are like the weather, only far more fickle. So, we must learn to live by faith, not by the ups and downs of our own emotional roller coasters.

Sometime during this day, you will probably be gripped by a strong negative emotion. Distrust it. Reign it in. Test it. And turn it over to God. Your emotions will inevitably change; God will not. So, trust Him completely as you watch your feelings slowly evaporate into thin air—which, of course, they will.

more stuff to think about

We are to live by faith, not feelings.

KAY ARTHUR

Discipleship is a decision to live by what I know about God,
not by what I feel about him or myself or my neighbors.

EUGENE PETERSON

Instead of waiting for the feeling, wait upon God.
You can do this by growing still and quiet, then expressing in
prayer what your mind knows is true about Him,
even if your heart doesn't feel it at this moment.

SHIRLEY DOBSON

The Big Idea

Feelings come and feelings go, but God never changes. So
when you have a choice between trusting your feelings or
trusting God, trust God.

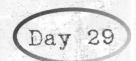

Learn God's Lessons
(Sooner Rather than Later)

Listen carefully to wisdom; set your mind on understanding.
Proverbs 2:2 NCV

One way that we learn about God is by learning the lessons that He is trying so desperately to teach us. But when it comes to learning God's lessons, most of us can be quite hardheaded. Why? Because we are, by nature, stubborn creatures; and because we seem destined, at times, to make things hard on ourselves.

As we go about the business of learning life's lessons, we can either do things the easy way or the hard way. The easy way can be summed up as follows: when God tries to teach us something, we learn it . . . the first time! Unfortunately, too many of us learn much more slowly than that.

When we resist God's instruction, He continues to teach, whether we like it or not. Our challenge, then, is to discern God's lessons from the experiences of everyday life. Hopefully, we learn those lessons sooner rather than later because the sooner we do so, the sooner He can move on to the next lesson and the next, and the next . . . .

more stuff to think about

The wise man gives proper appreciation in his life to
his past. He learns to sift the sawdust of heritage
in order to find the nuggets that make
the current moment have any meaning.

GRADY NUTT

The wonderful thing about God's schoolroom is that
we get to grade our own papers. You see,
He doesn't test us so He can learn how well we're doing.
He tests us so we can discover how well we're doing.

CHARLES SWINDOLL

A big difference exists between a head full of knowledge
and the words of God literally abiding in us.

BETH MOORE

The Big Idea

Would you like God's guidance? Then ask Him for it. When
you pray for guidance, God will give it (Luke 11:9). So ask.

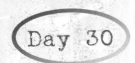

Day 30

Make the Most of the Time You've Been Given

Hard work means prosperity; only fools idle away their time.
PROVERBS 12:11 NLT

Time is a nonrenewable gift from God. But sometimes, we treat our time here on earth as if it were not a gift at all: We may be tempted to invest our lives in trivial pursuits and mindless diversions. But our Father in heaven wants us to do more . . . much more.

Are you one of those people who puts things off until the last minute? Do you waste time doing things that don't matter very much while putting off the important things until it's too late to do the job right? If so, it's now time to start making better choices.

It may seem like you've got all the time in the world to do the things you need to do, but time is shorter than you think. Time here on earth is limited . . . use it or lose it!

2 minutes A DAY

more stuff to think about

It is not fitting, when one is in God's service,
to have a gloomy face or a chilling look.

ST. FRANCIS OF ASSISI

This world is not our home, and we lament its sin-wrecked
condition, riddled with disease and death and distress.
But, for the growing of Christian character,
it is a proper training ground.

VANCE HAVNER

Our time is short! The time we can invest for God,
in creative things, in receiving our fellowmen
for Christ, is short!

BILLY GRAHAM

The Big Idea

If you don't value your time . . . neither will anybody else.

Look for Fulfillment in All the Right Places

I am the Gate. Anyone who goes through me will be cared for—will freely go in and out, and find pasture. A thief is only there to steal and kill and destroy. I came so they can have real and eternal life, more and better life than they ever dreamed of. "I am the Good Shepherd. The Good Shepherd puts the sheep before himself, sacrifices himself if necessary.

JOHN 10:9-11 MSG

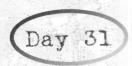

Where can we find fulfillment and contentment? Is it a result of wealth or power or beauty or fame? Hardly. Genuine contentment is a gift from God to those who trust Him and follow His commandments.

Our modern world seems preoccupied with the search for happiness. We are bombarded with messages telling us that happiness depends upon the acquisition of material possessions. These messages are false. Enduring peace is not the result of our acquisitions; it is a spiritual gift from God to those who obey Him and accept His will.

If we don't find contentment in God, we will never find it anywhere else. But, if we seek Him and obey Him, we will be blessed with an inner peace that is beyond human understanding. When God dwells at the center of our lives, peace and contentment will belong to us just as surely as we belong to God.

more stuff to think about

We are never more fulfilled than when our longing
for God is met by His presence in our lives.

BILLY GRAHAM

By trying to grab fulfillment everywhere, we find it nowhere.

ELISABETH ELLIOT

We will never be happy until we make God the source
of our fulfillment and the answer to our longings.

STORMIE OMARTIAN

The Big Idea

Contentment comes, not from your circumstances or your
possessions, but from your attitude. And remember this:
peace with God is the foundation of a contented life.

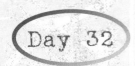

Day 32

Find the Courage to Follow God

Be strong and courageous, and do the work.
Don't be afraid or discouraged, for the LORD God, my God,
is with you. He won't leave you or forsake you.
1 CHRONICLES 28:20 HOLMAN CSB

B ecause we are saved by a risen Christ, we can have hope for the future, no matter how desperate our circumstances may seem. After all, God has promised that we are His throughout eternity. And, He has told us that we must place our hopes in Him.

Today, summon the courage to follow God. Even if the path seems difficult, even if your heart is fearful, trust your Heavenly Father and follow Him. Trust Him with your day and your life. Do His work, care for His children, and share His Good News. Let Him guide your steps. He will not lead you astray.

2 minutes A DAY

more stuff to think about

God of grace and God of glory, on Thy people pour
Thy power. Grant us wisdom; grant us courage
for the facing of this hour.

HARRY EMERSON FOSDICK

Dreaming the dream of God is not for cowards.

JOEY JOHNSON

Down through the centuries, in times of trouble and trial,
God has brought courage to the hearts of those who
love Him. The Bible is filled with assurances of God's help
and comfort in every kind of trouble which might
cause fears to arise in the human heart.
You can look ahead with promise, hope, and joy.

BILLY GRAHAM

The Big Idea

Is your courage being tested? Cling tightly to God's
promises, and pray. God can give you the strength to meet
any challenge, and that's exactly what you should ask Him
to do.

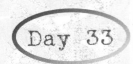

Follow Your Conscience

*Let us come near to God with a sincere heart and
a sure faith, because we have been made free from a
guilty conscience, and our bodies have
been washed with pure water.*

HEBREWS 10:22 NCV

God gave you a conscience for a very good reason: to make your path conform to His will. Billy Graham correctly observed, "Most of us follow our conscience as we follow a wheelbarrow. We push it in front of us in the direction we want to go." To do so, of course, is a profound mistake. Yet all of us, on occasion, have failed to listen to the voice that God planted in our hearts, and all of us have suffered the consequences.

Wise believers make it a practice to listen carefully to that quiet internal voice. Count yourself among that number. When your conscience speaks, listen and learn. In all likelihood, God is trying to get His message through. And in all likelihood, it is a message that you desperately need to hear.

2 minutes A DAY

more stuff to think about

The convicting work of the Holy Spirit awakens,
disturbs, and judges.

FRANKLIN GRAHAM

Spiritual life without guilt would be like physical life
without pain. Guilt is a defense mechanism; it's like an
alarm that goes off to lead you to confession when you sin.

JOHN MACARTHUR

A good conscience is a continual feast.

FRANCIS BACON

The Big Idea

Trust the quiet inner voice of your conscience: Treat your
conscience as you would a trusted advisor.

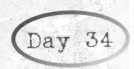

Day 34

Respect Your Body

Didn't you realize that your body is a sacred place, the place of the Holy Spirit? Don't you see that you can't live however you please, squandering what God paid such a high price for? The physical part of you is not some piece of property belonging to the spiritual part of you.

1 CORINTHIANS 6:19 MSG

If you're treating your body with respect, you're doing God's will. And if you're doing God's will, you'll have an easier time building a meaningful relationship with your Father in heaven. So, if you want to know God better, you should treat your body—and thus yourself—with respect. But sometimes, that's a hard thing to do.

You live in a society that is filled to the brim with temptations, distractions, and distortions about sex. You are bombarded with images that glamorize sex outside marriage. In fact, you are subjected to daily pressures and problems that were largely unknown to earlier generations.

So, do yourself a huge favor: treat yourself and your body with the respect it deserves. You deserve it, and so does God.

more stuff to think about

As you and I lay up for ourselves living, lasting treasures in
Heaven, we come to the awesome conclusion
that we ourselves are His treasure!

ANNE GRAHAM LOTZ

Let no one tell you that this body of ours is
a stranger to God.

ST. CYRIL OF JERUSALEM

Our body is a portable sanctuary through which we
are daily experiencing the presence of God.

RICHARD FOSTER

The Big Idea

You are incredibly special to God . . . Are you incredibly
special to yourself?

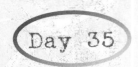

Put God in His Rightful Place

Do not worship any other gods besides me.
Exodus 20:3 NLT

If you really want to know God, you should start by putting Him first in your life. So here's a question worth thinking about: Have you made God your top priority by offering Him your heart, your soul, your talents, and your time? Or are you in the habit of giving God little more than a few hours on Sunday morning? The answer to these questions will determine, to a surprising extent, the quality of your life and the content of your character.

As you contemplate your own relationship with God, remember this: all of mankind is engaged in the practice of worship. Some folks choose to worship God and, as a result, reap the joy that He offers to His children. Other folks, folks who are stubbornly determined to do it "their way," distance themselves from God by worshiping such things as earthly possessions or personal gratification . . . and when they do, they suffer.

Does God rule your heart? If you sincerely want to know Him, you must answer yes—you must put your Creator in first place. No exceptions.

2 minutes a day

more stuff to think about

God wants to be in an intimate relationship with you.
He's the God who has orchestrated every event of your life
to give you the best chance to get to know Him, so that you
can experience the full measure of His love.

BILL HYBELS

When we are in the presence of God, removed from
distractions, we are able to hear him more clearly,
and a secure environment has been established for
the young and broken places in our hearts to surface.

JOHN ELDREDGE

The Big Idea

Today, spend a few minutes thinking about your relationship
with God. Is it really an intimate one-on-one connection,
or are you allowing other things to come between you and
your Creator? Write down three specific steps that you can
take right now to forge a stronger bond with your Heavenly
Father.

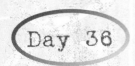

Trust God's Wisdom

*Understanding is like a fountain which gives life
to those who use it.*
Proverbs 16:22 NCV

The world has its own brand of wisdom, a brand of wisdom that is often wrong and sometimes dangerous. God, on the other hand, has a different brand of wisdom, a wisdom that will lead you closer to Him.

Where will you place your trust today? Will you trust in the wisdom of fallible men and women, or will you place your faith in God's perfect wisdom? The answer to this question will determine the direction of your day and the quality of your decisions.

Are you tired? Discouraged? Fearful? Be comforted and trust God. Are you worried or anxious? Be confident in God's power. Are you confused? Listen to the quiet voice of your Heavenly Father—He is not a God of confusion. Talk with Him; listen to Him; trust Him. His wisdom, unlike the "wisdom" of the world, will never let you down.

2 minutes a DAY

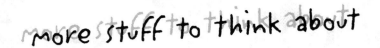
more stuff to think about

Life isn't life without some divine decisions that
our mortal minds simply cannot comprehend.

BETH MOORE

Most of us go through life praying a little, planning a little,
jockeying for position, hoping but never being quite certain
of anything, and always secretly afraid that we will miss the
way. This is a tragic waste of truth and never gives rest to
the heart. There is a better way. It is to repudiate our own
wisdom and take instead the infinite wisdom of God.

A. W. TOZER

The center of power is not to be found in summit meetings or
in peace conferences. It is not in Peking or Washington
or the United Nations, but rather where a child
of God prays in the power of the Spirit for God's will
to be done in her life, in her home,
and in the world around her.

RUTH BELL GRAHAM

The Big Idea

When life seems unfair, try spending more time trusting God
and less time dwelling on "the unfairness of it all."

GOD

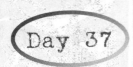

The Wisdom of Kindness

Kind people do themselves a favor, but cruel people bring trouble on themselves.
PROVERBS 11:17 NCV

If we believe the words of Proverbs 11:17—and we should—then we understand that kindness is its own reward. And, if we obey the commandments of our Savior—and we should—we must sow seeds of kindness wherever we go.

Kindness, compassion, and forgiveness are hallmarks of our Christian faith. So today, in honor of the One who first showed compassion for us, let's teach our families and friends the art of kindness through our words and through our deeds. Our loved ones are watching . . . and so is God.

more stuff to think about

As you're rushing through life, take time to stop a moment,
look into people's eyes, say something kind,
and try to make them laugh!

BARBARA JOHNSON

The nicest thing we can do for our heavenly Father
is to be kind to one of His children.

ST. TERESA OF AVILA

No one heals himself by wounding another.

AMBROSE OF MILAN

The Big Idea

You can't just talk about it: In order to be a kind person,
you must not only think kind thoughts, you must also do
kind things. So get busy! The best day to become a more
generous person is this day!

Be Thankful

Praise the LORD. Give thanks to the LORD, for he is good;
his love endures forever.
PSALM 106:1 NIV

A re you basically a thankful person? Do you appreciate the stuff you've got and the life that you're privileged to live? You most certainly should be thankful. After all, when you stop to think about it, God has given you more blessings than you can count. So the question of the day is this: will you slow down long enough to thank your Heavenly Father . . . or not?

Sometimes, life here on earth can be complicated, demanding, and frustrating. When the demands of life leave you rushing from place to place with scarcely a moment to spare, you may fail to pause and thank your Creator for the countless blessings He has given you. Failing to thank God is understandable . . . but it's wrong.

So here's something to remember: when it comes to knowing God, a thankful, humble heart isn't just helpful; it's essential.

2 MINUTES A DAY

more stuff to think about

The best way to show my gratitude to God is to
accept everything, even my problems, with joy.

MOTHER TERESA

Gratitude to God makes even a temporal blessing
a taste of heaven.

WILLIAM ROMAINE

Prayer is a burst of love, a look to heaven, a cry of thanks.

ST. THÉRÈSE OF LISIEUX

The Big Idea

Don't overlook God's gifts. Every sunrise represents yet
another beautifully wrapped gift from God. Unwrap it;
treasure it; use it; and give thanks to the Giver.

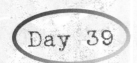

Keep Your Priorities in Line with God's Priorities

Come near to God, and God will come near to you.
You sinners, clean sin out of your lives. You who
are trying to follow God and the world at the same time,
make your thinking pure.

JAMES 4:8 NCV

Have you fervently asked God to help prioritize your life? Have you asked Him for guidance and for the courage to do the things that you know need to be done? If so, then you're continually inviting your Creator to reveal Himself in a variety of ways. As a follower of Christ, you must do no less.

When you make God's priorities your priorities, you will receive God's abundance and His peace. When you make God a full partner in every aspect of your life, He will lead you along the proper path: His path. When you allow God to reign over your heart, He will honor you with spiritual blessings that are simply too numerous to count. So, as you plan for the day ahead, make God's will your ultimate priority. When you do, every other priority will have a tendency to fall neatly into place.

more stuff to think about

Until your purpose lines up with God's purpose,
you will never be happy or fulfilled.

CHARLES STANLEY

Like Jesus in his time on earth, you must set priorities,
choose from among many good causes that vie for
your attention, and seek to do what will be most effective
for the advancement of God's rule.

STANLEY GRENZ

With God, it's never "Plan B" or "second best."
It's always "Plan A." And, if we let Him,
He'll make something beautiful of our lives.

GLORIA GAITHER

The Big Idea

Setting priorities may mean saying no. You don't have time
to do everything, so it's perfectly okay to say no to the things
that mean less so that you'll have time for the things that
mean more.

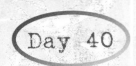

Be on Guard Against Temptation

Watch and pray so that you will not fall into temptation.
The spirit is willing but the body is weak.
MATTHEW 26:41 NIV

In a letter to believers, Peter offers a stern warning: "Your adversary, the devil, prowls around like a roaring lion, seeking someone to devour" (1 Peter 5:8 NASB). What was true in New Testament times is equally true in our own. Satan tempts his prey and then devours them (and it's up to you—and only you—to make sure that you're not one of the ones being devoured!).

As a dues-paying citizen of the 21st century, you're aware that temptations are everywhere. Satan is determined to win; you must be equally determined that he does not.

2 minutes a day

more stuff to think about

Jesus faced every temptation known to humanity
so that He could identify with us.

BETH MOORE

Ask Christ to come into your heart to forgive you
and help you. When you do, Christ will take up residence in
your life by His Holy Spirit, and when you face temptations
and trials, you will no longer face them alone.

BILLY GRAHAM

It is not the Word hidden in the head that keeps us from sin.
It is the Word hidden in the heart.

VANCE HAVNER

The Big Idea

You live in a temptation generation—you can find temptation
in lots of places. Your job is to avoid those places!

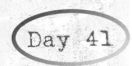

Entrusting Your Hopes to God

*You, Lord, give true peace to those who depend on you,
because they trust you.*

ISAIAH 26:3 NCV

Have you ever felt hope for the future slipping away? If so, you have temporarily lost sight of the hope that we, as believers, must place in the promises of our Heavenly Father. If you are feeling discouraged, worried, or worse, remember the words of Psalm 31:24: "Be of good courage, and He shall strengthen your heart, all you who hope in the LORD" (NKJV).

Of course, we will face disappointments and failures, but these are only temporary defeats. Of course, this world can be a place of trials and tribulations, but we are secure. God has promised us peace, joy, and eternal life. And God keeps His promises today, tomorrow, and forever.

more stuff to think about

The will of God is the most delicious
and delightful thing in the universe.
HANNAH WHITALL SMITH

God's purposes are often hidden from us.
He owes us no explanations.
We owe Him our complete love and trust.
WARREN WIERSBE

It is more serious to lose hope than to sin.
JOHN OF CARPATHOS

The Big Idea

Never be afraid to hope—or to ask—for a miracle.

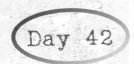

Get Beyond the Distractions

If you decide for God, living a life of God-worship, it follows that you don't fuss about what's on the table at mealtimes or whether the clothes in your closet are in fashion. There is far more to your life than the food you put in your stomach, more to your outer appearance than the clothes you hang on your body.

MATTHEW 6:25 MSG

All of us must live through those days when the traffic jams, the computer crashes, and the dog makes a main course out of the homework. But, when we find ourselves distracted by the minor frustrations of life, we must catch ourselves, take a deep breath, and lift our thoughts upward.

Although we may, at times, struggle mightily to rise above the distractions of everyday living, we need never struggle alone. God is here—eternal and faithful, with infinite patience and love—and, if we reach out to Him, He will restore our sense of perspective and give peace to our souls.

more stuff to think about

Whatever we focus on determines what we become.

E. STANLEY JONES

In the Garden of Gethsemane, Jesus went through
agony of soul in His efforts to resist the temptation
to do what He felt like doing rather than
what He knew was God's will for Him.

JOYCE MEYER

There is an enormous power in little things
to distract our attention from God.

OSWALD CHAMBERS

The Big Idea

Take a few minutes to consider the everyday distractions
that are interfering with your life and your faith. Then, jot
down at least three ideas for minimizing those distractions or
eliminating them altogether.

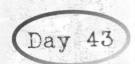

Day 43

Make Your Actions Conform to Your Beliefs

Therefore by their fruits you will know them.
MATTHEW 7:20 NKJV

English clergyman Thomas Fuller observed, "He does not believe who does not live according to his beliefs." These words are most certainly true. We may proclaim our beliefs to our hearts' content, but our proclamations will mean nothing—to others or to ourselves—unless we accompany our words with deeds that match. The sermons that we live are far more compelling than the ones we preach.

Like it or not, your life is an accurate reflection of your creed. If this fact gives you some cause for concern, don't bother talking about the changes that you intend to make—make them. And then, when your good deeds speak for themselves—as they most certainly will—don't interrupt.

2 minutes a day

more stuff to think about

It is only by fidelity in little things that a true and
constant love of God can be distinguished from
a passing fervor of spirit.

FRANÇOIS FÈNELON

It is less important to ask a Christian what he or she believes
about the Bible than to inquire what he or she does with it.

LESSLIE NEWBIGIN

What you do reveals what you believe about God,
regardless of what you say. When God reveals what He has
purposed to do, you face a crisis—a decision time.
God and the world can tell from your response
what you really believe about God.

HENRY BLACKABY

The Big Idea

Talking about your beliefs is easy. But, making your actions
match your words is much harder. Nevertheless, if you really
want to be honest with yourself, then you must make your
actions match your beliefs. Period.

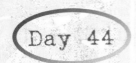

In Love with Stuff?

*Yes, a person is a fool to store up earthly wealth
but not have a rich relationship with God.*

LUKE 12:21 NLT

Are you overly concerned with the stuff that money
can buy? If so, here's a word of warning: your love
for material possessions is getting in the way of your
relationship with God.

Up on the stage of life, material possessions should
play a rather small role. Of course, we all need the basic
necessities like food, clothing, and a place to live. But once
we've met those needs, the piling up of possessions creates
more problems than it solves. Our real riches, of course, are
not of this world. We're never really rich until we are rich in
spirit.

So here's a bit of advice that you must take very
seriously: don't love stuff, love God. When you do, you'll
be rewarded, and you'll be blessed, now and throughout
eternity.

more stuff to think about

The cross is laid on every Christian. It begins with the call to abandon the attachments of this world.

DIETRICH BONHOEFFER

As faithful stewards of what we have, ought we not to give earnest thought to our staggering surplus?

ELISABETH ELLIOT

There is absolutely no evidence that complexity and materialism lead to happiness. On the contrary, there is plenty of evidence that simplicity and spirituality lead to joy, a blessedness that is better than happiness.

DENNIS SWANBERG

The Big Idea

The world wants you to believe that "money and stuff" can buy happiness. Don't believe it! Genuine happiness comes not from money, but from the things that money can't buy—starting, of course, with your relationship to God and His only begotten Son.

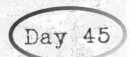

Day 45

Trust God's Promises

Patient endurance is what you need now,
so you will continue to do God's will.
Then you will receive all that he has promised.

HEBREWS 10:36 NLT

God has made quite a few promises to you, and He intends to keep every single one of them. You will find these promises in a book like no other: the Holy Bible. The Bible is your roadmap for life here on earth and for life eternal—as a believer, you are called upon to trust its promises, to follow its commandments, and to share its Good News.

God has made promises to all of humanity and to you. God's promises never fail and they never grow old. You must trust those promises and share them with your family, with your friends, and with the world . . . starting now . . . and ending never.

more stuff to think about

The stars may fall, but God's promises will stand
and be fulfilled.

J. I. PACKER

The promises of Scripture are not mere pious hopes or
sanctified guesses. They are more than sentimental words to
be printed on decorated cards for Sunday School children.
They are eternal verities. They are true.
There is no perhaps about them.

PETER MARSHALL

There are four words I wish we would never forget,
and they are, "God keeps his word."

CHARLES SWINDOLL

The Big Idea

Do you really trust God's promises, or are you hedging your
bets? Today, think about the role that God's Word plays in
your life, and think about ways that you can worry less and
trust God more.

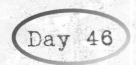

Have a Healthy Fear of God

Since we are receiving a Kingdom that cannot be destroyed,
let us be thankful and please God by worshiping him
with holy fear and awe.

HEBREWS 12:28 NLT

D o you have a healthy, fearful respect for God's power? If so, you are both wise and obedient. And, because you are a thoughtful believer, you also understand that genuine wisdom begins with a profound appreciation for God's limitless power.

God praises humility and punishes pride. That's why God's greatest servants will always be those humble men and women who care less for their own glory and more for God's glory. In God's kingdom, the only way to achieve greatness is to shun it. And the only way to be wise is to understand these facts: God is great; He is all-knowing; and He is all-powerful. We must respect Him, and we must humbly obey His commandments, or we must accept the consequences of our misplaced pride.

more stuff to think about

A healthy fear of God will do much to deter us from sin.

CHARLES SWINDOLL

When true believers are awed by the greatness of God
and by the privilege of becoming His children,
then they become sincerely motivated, effective evangelists.

BILL HYBELS

It is not possible that mortal men should be thoroughly
conscious of the divine presence without being
filled with awe.

C. H. SPURGEON

The Big Idea

Your respect for God should make you fearful of disobeying
Him . . . very fearful.

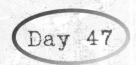

Take the Positive Path

But the path of the just is like the shining sun, that shines ever brighter unto the perfect day. The way of the wicked is like darkness; they do not know what makes them stumble.

PROVERBS 4:18-19 NKJV

When Jesus addressed His disciples, He warned that each one must, "take up his cross and follow me." The disciples must have known exactly what the Master meant. In Jesus' day, prisoners were forced to carry their own crosses to the location where they would be put to death. Thus, Christ's message was clear: in order to follow Him, Christ's disciples must deny themselves and, instead, trust Him completely. Nothing has changed since then.

If we are to be dutiful disciples of the One from Galilee, we must trust Him and we must follow Him. Jesus never comes "next." He is always first. He shows us the path of life.

Do you seek to be a worthy disciple of Jesus? Then pick up His cross today and follow in His footsteps. When you do, you can walk with confidence: He will never lead you astray.

2 minutes A DAY

more stuff to think about

Teach a man a rule and you help him solve a problem;
teach a man to walk with God and you help him
solve the rest of his life.

JOHN ELDREDGE

A holy life will produce the deepest impression.
Lighthouses blow no horns; they only shine.

D. L. MOODY

Be such a person, and live such a life, that if every person
were such as you, and every life a life like yours,
this earth would be God's Paradise.

PHILLIPS BROOKS

The Big Idea

When it comes to telling the world about your relationship
with God, your actions speak much more loudly than your
words . . . so behave accordingly.

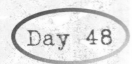

Transformed?

You have been born again, and this new life did not come from something that dies, but from something that cannot die. You were born again through God's living message that continues forever.

2 PETER 1:23 NCV

God's Word is clear: When we genuinely invite Him to reign over our hearts, and when we accept His transforming love, we are forever changed. When we welcome Christ into our hearts, an old life ends and a new way of living—along with a completely new way of viewing the world—begins.

Each morning offers a fresh opportunity to invite Christ, yet once again, to rule over our hearts and our days. Each morning presents yet another opportunity to take up His cross and follow in His footsteps. Today, let us rejoice in the new life that is ours through Christ, and let us follow Him, step by step, on the path that He first walked.

2 minutes A DAY

more stuff to think about

God wants to revolutionize our lives—by showing us how knowing Him can be the most powerful force to help us become all we want to be.

BILL HYBELS

Once grace has scrubbed the soul, anyone can take their place in the lineage of the Son of God.

CALVIN MILLER

You were born with tremendous potential.
When you were born again through faith in Jesus Christ, God added spiritual gifts to your natural talents.

WARREN WIERSBE

The Big Idea

A true conversion experience results in a life transformed by Christ and a commitment to following in His footsteps.

Discouraged?

Do not be afraid or discouraged.
For the LORD your God is with you wherever you go.
JOSHUA 1:9 NLT

Even the most devout Christians can become discouraged, and you are no exception. After all, you live in a world where expectations can be high and demands can be even higher.

If you find yourself enduring difficult circumstances, don't lose hope. If you face uncertainties about the future, don't become anxious. And if you become discouraged with the direction of your day or your life, don't despair. Instead, lift your thoughts and prayers to your Heavenly Father. He is a God of possibility, not negativity. You can be sure that He will guide you through your difficulties and beyond them . . . far beyond.

So here's the moral to the story: God is always with you, He's going to protect you, and because He is always faithful, you can live courageously today and every day of your life.

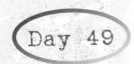

more stuff to think about

Working in the vineyard,
Working all the day,
Never be discouraged,
Only watch and pray.

FANNY CROSBY

All discouragement is of the devil.

HANNAH WHITALL SMITH

The most profane word we use is "hopeless."
When you say a situation or person is hopeless,
you are slamming the door in the face of God.

KATHY TROCCOLI

The Big Idea

If you're feeling discouraged, try to redirect your thoughts
away from the troubles that plague you—focus, instead,
upon the opportunities that surround you.

Pop Quiz

Grow in grace and understanding of our Master and Savior,
Jesus Christ. Glory to the Master, now and forever! Yes!
2 PETER 3:18 MSG

Okay, you're at day 50 of this book (which means you're half-way through). So here's a pop quiz (think of it as a mini mid-term) that will help you gauge the level of your spiritual health:

1. Do you attend your church regularly?
2. Are you a builder of bridges inside the four walls of your church and outside those walls?
3. Do you contribute to God's kingdom by contributing your time and your talents?
4. Do you spend time each day in studying your Bible, praying, and generally getting to know God?

If you answered these questions in the affirmative, then you are well on your way to a closer relationship with your Creator—and you passed your mid-term exam with flying colors.

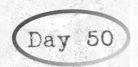

2 MINUTES A DAY

more stuff to think about

We do the works, but God works in us
in the doing of the works.

St. Augustine

My heart's desire is to find more opportunities
to give myself away and teach my children the joy
of service at the same time.

Liz Curtis Higgs

In the very place where God has put us,
whatever its limitations, whatever kind of work it may be,
we may indeed serve the Lord Christ.

Elisabeth Elliot

The Big Idea

If you seek the things that God values, you will be satisfied;
if you seek the things that the world values, you will be
disappointed.

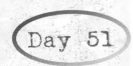

Make the Most of Whatever Comes

A man's heart plans his way,
but the LORD determines his steps.

PROVERBS 16:9 HOLMAN CSB

Sometimes, we must accept life on its terms, not our own. When events transpire that are beyond our control, we have a choice: we can either learn the art of acceptance, or we can make ourselves miserable as we struggle to change the unchangeable.

We must entrust the things we cannot change to God. Once we have done so, we can prayerfully and faithfully tackle the important work that He has placed before us: doing something about the things we can change . . . and doing it sooner rather than later.

So if you've encountered unfortunate circumstances that are beyond your power to control, accept those circumstances . . . and trust God. When you do, you can be comforted in the knowledge that your Creator is both loving and wise, and that He understands His plans perfectly, even when you do not.

more stuff to think about

Do all the good you can. By all the means you can.
In all the ways you can. In all the places you can.
At all the times you can. To all the people you can.
As long as ever you can.

JOHN WESLEY

Never use your problem as an excuse for
bad attitudes or behavior.

JOYCE MEYER

Great opportunities often disguise themselves in small tasks.

RICK WARREN

The Big Idea

Acceptance means learning to trust God more. Today, think
of at least one aspect of your life that you've been reluctant
to accept, and then prayerfully ask God to help you trust
Him more by accepting the past.

Ready to Move Mountains?

*For truly I say to you, if you have faith as a mustard seed,
you shall say to this mountain, "Move from here to there"
and it shall move; and nothing shall be impossible to you.*

MATTHEW 17:20 NASB

Because we live in a demanding world, all of us have mountains to climb and mountains to move. Moving those mountains requires faith.

Are you a mountain-moving Christian whose faith is evident for all to see? Or, are you a spiritual underachiever? As you think about the answer to that question, consider this: God needs more people who are willing to move mountains for His glory and for His kingdom.

Are you willing to let God help you move mountains, or are you still stumbling around over a few little molehills? The answer should be obvious. And so, with no more delays, let the mountain moving begin.

more stuff to think about

Faith never knows where it is being led,
but it loves and knows the One Who is leading.

OSWALD CHAMBERS

We are never stronger than the moment
we admit we are weak.

BETH MOORE

Great hopes make great men.

THOMAS FULLER

The Big Idea

If you don't have faith, you'll never move mountains. But if
you do have faith, there's no limit to the things that you and
God, working together, can accomplish.

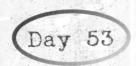
Take a Look at God's Creation

You are the God of miracles and wonders!
You demonstrate your awesome power among the nations.
PSALM 77:14 NLT

If you're trying to get to know God better, it helps to look carefully at all the stuff He has made.

If you're paying careful attention to God's amazing handiwork, you're to be congratulated. But if you've stopped paying attention to the incredible things that are happening around you, it's time to slow down long enough to open your eyes—and your heart—to God.

Do you have faith that God can work miracles in your own life? Hopefully so. But, if you have allowed yourself to become a "doubting Thomas," you are attempting to place limitations on a God who has none. Instead of doubting your Heavenly Father, you must trust Him. Then, you must wait and watch . . . because something miraculous is going to happen to you, and it might just happen today.

more stuff to think about

The universe is but one vast symbol of God.

THOMAS CARLYLE

The world, space, and all visible components reverberate
with God's Presence and demonstrate His Mighty Power.

FRANKLIN GRAHAM

Because God created the Natural—invented it out of
His love and artistry—it demands our reverence.

C. S. LEWIS

The Big Idea

Don't miss the miracle of God's creation . . . it's all around
you.

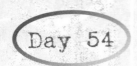

Day 54

Understand the Importance of Character

May integrity and uprightness protect me,
because my hope is in you.
PSALM 25:21 NIV

It has been said that character is what we are when nobody is watching. How true. But, as Bill Hybels correctly observed, "Every secret act of character, conviction, and courage has been observed in living color by our omniscient God." And isn't that a sobering thought?

When we do things that we know aren't right, we try to hide our misdeeds from family members and friends. But even then, God is watching.

If you sincerely wish to walk with God, you must seek, to the best of your ability, to follow His commandments. When you do, your character will take care of itself . . . and you won't need to look over your shoulder to see who, besides God, is watching.

more stuff to think about

Maintaining your integrity in a world of sham is
no small accomplishment.

WAYNE OATES

Often, our character is at greater risk in prosperity
than in adversity.

BETH MOORE

Character is formed by doing the thing we are
supposed to do, when it should be done,
whether we feel like doing it or not.

FATHER FLANAGAN

The Big Idea

Talking about your beliefs is easy. But, making your actions
match your words is much harder. Nevertheless, if you really
want to be honest with yourself, then you must make your
actions match your beliefs. Period.

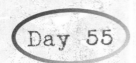

Day 55

Stewardship of God's Gifts

*God has given gifts to each of you from his great variety of
spiritual gifts. Manage them well so that
God's generosity can flow through you.*

1 PETER 4:10 NLT

D o you want to be a faithful follower of Christ? Do
you want to know God's will for your life? And do
you trust God's promises? If so, then you will be a
faithful steward of the gifts He has given you.

When you are a reliable steward of your talents,
and when you give God that which is rightfully His, you
experience the spiritual growth that always accompanies
obedience to the Creator. But, if you attempt to shortchange
God, either materially or spiritually, you will inevitably
distance yourself from Him.

Everybody has special gifts, and you are no exception.
Today, accept this challenge: value the talent that God has
given you, nourish it, make it grow, and share it with the
world. Manage your resources as if they were a one-of-a-
kind treasure on loan from God, which, by the way, they are.

more stuff to think about

Jesus had much to say about money, . . .
more than about almost any other subject.

BILL BRIGHT

All the blessings we enjoy are divine deposits,
committed to our trust on this condition:
that they should be dispensed for the benefit
of our neighbors.

JOHN CALVIN

You are the only person on earth who can use your ability.

ZIG ZIGLAR

The Big Idea

When you become a better steward of the resources God
has given you . . . He gives you more resources to manage.

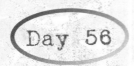

Live on Purpose

God chose you to be his people,
so I urge you now to live the life to which God called you.
EPHESIANS 4:1 NCV

L ife is best lived on purpose. And purpose, like
everything else in the universe, begins with God.
Whether you realize it or not, God has a plan for your
life, a divine calling, a direction in which He is leading you.
When you welcome God into your heart and establish a
genuine relationship with Him, He will begin, in time, to
make His purposes known.

Sometimes, God's intentions will be clear to you; other
times, God's plan will seem uncertain at best. But even on
those difficult days when you are unsure which way to turn,
you must never lose sight of these overriding facts: God
created you for a reason; He has important work for you to
do; and He's waiting patiently for you to do it.

And the next step is up to you.

2 minutes A DAY

more stuff to think about

The really committed leave the safety of the harbor,
accept the risk of the open seas of faith, and set their
compasses for the place of total devotion to God and
whatever life adventures He plans for them.

BILL HYBELS

You can believe in Jesus Christ as your Savior,
make heaven and miss hell, but never realize the power
that God intended for you to know in this life.

ANGELA THOMAS

The Big Idea

Discovering God's purpose for your life requires a
willingness to be open. God's plan is unfolding day by day.
If you keep your eyes and your heart open, He'll reveal
His plans. God has big things in store for you, but He may
have quite a few lessons to teach you before you are fully
prepared to do His will and fulfill His purposes.

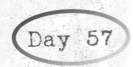

Worship Together

*Let's see how inventive we can be in encouraging love and
helping out, not avoiding worshipping together
as some do but spurring each other on.*
HEBREWS 10:24-25 MSG

Every believer—including you—needs to be part
of a community of faith. Your association with
fellow Christians should be uplifting, enlightening,
encouraging, and consistent.

Are you an active member of your fellowship? Are you
a builder of bridges inside the four walls of your church and
outside it? Do you contribute your time and your talents to
a close-knit band of hope-filled believers? Hopefully so.
The fellowship of believers is intended to be a powerful tool
for spreading God's Good News and uplifting His children.
God intends for you to be a fully contributing member of
that fellowship. Your intentions should be the same.

more stuff to think about

Every time a new person comes to God, every time
someone's gifts find expression in the fellowship of believers,
every time a family in need is surrounded by the caring
church, the truth is affirmed anew:
the Church triumphant is alive and well!

GLORIA GAITHER

Authentic worship flows out of telling the truth,
out of facing our greatest fears, out of finding peace in
unexpected places.

SHEILA WALSH

Because his spiritual existence transcends form, matter,
and location, we have the freedom to worship him and
experience his indwelling presence wherever we are.

R. C. SPROUL

The Big Idea

Worship reminds you of the awesome power of God. So
worship Him daily, and allow Him to work through you every
day of the week (not just on Sunday).

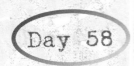

Day 58

Love God and Get Busy

So don't get tired of doing what is good.
Don't get discouraged and give up, for we will reap
a harvest of blessing at the appropriate time.

GALATIANS 6:9 NLT

The old saying is both familiar and true: actions speak louder than words. And as believers, we must beware: our actions should always give credence to the changes that Christ can make in the lives of those who walk with Him.

God calls upon each of us to act in accordance with His will and with respect for His commandments. If we are to be responsible believers, we must realize that it is never enough simply to hear the instructions of God; we must also live by them. And it is never enough to wait idly by while others do God's work here on earth; we, too, must act. Doing God's work is a responsibility that each of us must bear, and when we do, our loving Heavenly Father rewards our efforts with a bountiful harvest.

2 minutes a day

more stuff to think about

Remember that the Christian life is one of action, not of speech and daydreams. Let there be few words and many deeds, and let them be done willingly.

VINCENT PALLOTTI

Blessed are those who know what on earth they are here on earth to do and set themselves about the business of doing it.

MAX LUCADO

Does God care about all the responsibilities we have to juggle in our daily lives? Of course. But he cares more that our lives demonstrate balance, the ability to discern what is essential and give ourselves fully to it.

PENELOPE STOKES

The Big Idea

As the old saying goes, there are three kinds of people: people who make things happen, people who wait for things to happen, and people who scratch their heads and ask, "What happened?" You should be the kind of person who makes things happen.

Since Tomorrow Is Not Promised, Serve God Now

We must do the works of Him who sent Me while it is day.
Night is coming when no one can work.

JOHN 9:4 HOLMAN CSB

The words of John 9:4 remind us that "night is coming" for all of us. But until then, God gives us each day and fills it to the brim with possibilities. The day is presented to us fresh and clean at midnight, free of charge, but we must beware: Today is a non-renewable resource—once it's gone, it's gone forever. Our responsibility, of course, is to use this day in the service of God's will and in accordance with His commandments.

Today, treasure the time that God has given you. And search for the hidden possibilities that God has placed along your path. This day is a priceless gift from your Creator, so use it joyfully and productively. And encourage others to do likewise. After all, night is coming when no one can work . . .

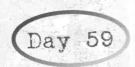

2 minutes A DAY

more stuff to think about

An early walk and talk with the Lord will last all day.
ANONYMOUS

I beg you do not squander life.
And don't live for this world only.
BILLY GRAHAM

Live in such a way that any day would make a suitable
capstone for life. Live so that you need not change your
mode of living, even if your sudden departure were
immediately predicted to you.
C. H. SPURGEON

The Big Idea

Jesus was a servant, and if you want to follow Him, you must
be a servant, too—even when service requires sacrifice.

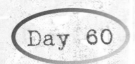

God Can Handle It

So, you see, it is impossible to please God without faith. Anyone who wants to come to him must believe that there is a God and that he rewards those who sincerely seek him.

HEBREWS 11:6 NLT

Every life—including yours—is a series of wins and losses. Every step of the way, through every triumph and tragedy, God walks with you, ready and willing to strengthen you. So the next time you find your courage tested to the limit, remember to take your fears to God. If you call upon Him, you will be comforted. Whatever your challenge, whatever your trouble, God can handle it.

When you place your faith, your trust, indeed your life in the hands of your Heavenly Father, you'll be amazed at the marvelous things He can do with you and through you. So, strengthen your faith through praise, through worship, through Bible study, and through prayer. And trust God's plans. With Him, all things are possible, and He stands ready to open a world of possibilities to you . . . if you have faith.

2 minutes A DAY

more stuff to think about

Faith is always tested for three reasons: to prove whether
our faith is real; to help our faith grow;
and to bring glory to the Lord.

WARREN WIERSBE

He treats us as sons, and all he asks in return is that we shall
treat Him as a Father whom we can trust without anxiety.
We must take the son's place of dependence and trust,
and we must let Him keep the father's place of
care and responsibility.

HANNAH WHITALL SMITH

The task ahead of us is never as great as
the Power behind us.

ANONYMOUS

The Big Idea

If you'd like infinite protection, there's only one place you
can receive it: from an infinite God. So remember: when you
live in the center of God's will, you will also be living in the
center of God's protection.

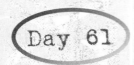

Day 61

Spiritual Maturity, Day by Day

When I was a child, I spoke and thought and reasoned as a child does. But when I grew up, I put away childish things.

1 CORINTHIANS 13:11 NLT

The path to spiritual maturity unfolds day by day. Each day offers the opportunity to worship God, to ignore God, or to rebel against God. When we worship Him with our prayers, our words, our thoughts, and our actions, we are blessed by the richness of our relationship with the Father. But if we ignore God altogether or intentionally rebel against His commandments, we rob ourselves of His blessings.

Today offers yet another opportunity for spiritual growth. If you choose, you can seize that opportunity by obeying God's Word, by seeking His will, and by walking with His Son.

2 minutes A DAY

more stuff to think about

The born-again Christian sees life not as a blurred,
confused, meaningless mass,
but as something planned and purposeful.

BILLY GRAHAM

God's goal is that we move toward maturity—
all our past failures and faults notwithstanding.

CHARLES SWINDOLL

The journey to discover your purpose in life starts at home.

CRISWELL FREEMAN

The Big Idea

Spiritual maturity is a journey, not a destination.

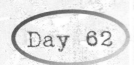

Be Disciplined

*But I discipline my body and bring it into subjection,
lest, when I have preached to others,
I myself should become disqualified.*

1 Corinthians 9:27 NKJV

Are you a self-disciplined person? If so, congratulations . . . your disciplined approach to life can help you build a more meaningful relationship with God. Why? Because God expects all His believers (including you) to lead lives of disciplined obedience to Him . . . and He rewards those believers who do.

God doesn't reward laziness, misbehavior, or apathy. God is less concerned with your party time than He is with your prayer time. And God wants all His followers (including you) to behave with dignity and self-control.

So, if you want to know God a little better, try becoming a more disciplined person. When you do, you'll be rewarded—richly rewarded—for your efforts.

2 minutes A DAY

more stuff to think about

As we seek to become disciples of Jesus Christ,
we should never forget that the word *disciple* is directly
related to the word *discipline*. To be a disciple of
the Lord Jesus Christ is to know his discipline.

DENNIS SWANBERG

Man's great danger is the combination of
his increased control over the elements
and his lack of control over himself.

ALBERT SCHWEITZER

Personal humility is a spiritual discipline
and the hallmark of the service of Jesus.

FRANKLIN GRAHAM

The Big Idea

A disciplined lifestyle gives you more control: The more
disciplined you become, the more you can take control over
your life (which, by the way, is far better than letting your life
take control over you).

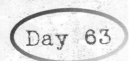

Hang Out
with Wise People

He who walks with the wise grows wise. . . .
PROVERBS 13:20 NIV

Are you and your friends wise guys and girls? And, are you striving to help each other become a little wiser every day? Hopefully so.

All of us would like to be wise, but not all of us are willing to do the work that is required to become wise. Why? Because wisdom isn't free—it takes time and effort to acquire.

To become wise, we must seek God's wisdom and live according to His Word. To become wise, we must seek wisdom with consistency and purpose. To become wise, we must not only learn the lessons of the Christian life, we must also live by them (and hang out with people who do likewise).

If you sincerely desire to become wise—and if you seek to share your hard-earned wisdom with others—your actions must give credence to your words. The best way to share one's wisdom—perhaps the only way—is not by words, but by example.

2 minutes A DAY

Wisdom is like a savings account: If you add to it consistently, then eventually you'll have a great sum. The secret to success is consistency. Do you seek wisdom? Then seek it every day, and seek it in the right place. That place, of course, is, first and foremost, the Word of God.

The next best thing to being wise oneself is to live
in a circle of those who are.

C. S. LEWIS

One of the ways God refills us after failure is through the blessing of Christian fellowship. Just experiencing the joy of simple activities shared with other children of God can have a healing effect on us.

ANNE GRAHAM LOTZ

The Big Idea

If your friends consistently encourage you to become a better person, be grateful. If your friends consistently encourage you to do things you're not proud of, find new friends.

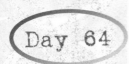

Be Careful How You Direct Your Thoughts

Finally, brothers, whatever is true, whatever is noble, whatever is right, whatever is pure, whatever is lovely, whatever is admirable—if anything is excellent or praiseworthy—think about such things.

PHILIPPIANS 4:8 NIV

If you really want to get to know God, you'll need to take charge of your thoughts before the world takes charge of them. How will you direct your thoughts today? Will you obey the words of Philippians 4:8 by dwelling upon those things that are true, admirable, and worthy of praise? Or will you allow your thoughts to be hijacked by the negativity that seems to dominate our troubled world.

God intends that you be an ambassador for Him, an enthusiastic, hope-filled Christian. But God won't force you to adopt a positive attitude. It's up to you to think positively about your blessings and opportunities . . . or not.

So, today and every day hereafter, celebrate this life that God has given you by focusing your thoughts and your energies upon things that are excellent and praiseworthy. Count your blessings instead of your hardships. And thank the Giver of all things good for gifts that are simply too numerous to count.

more stuff to think about

Make yourselves nests of pleasant thoughts.

JOHN RUSKIN

I became aware of one very important concept
I had missed before: my attitude—not my circumstances—
was what was making me unhappy.

VONETTE BRIGHT

It is the thoughts and intents of the heart that
shape a person's life.

JOHN ELDREDGE

The Big Idea

Good thoughts can lead you to some very good places . . .
and bad thoughts can lead elsewhere. So guard your
thoughts accordingly.

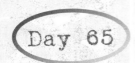

Holiness Before Happiness

Blessed are those who hunger and thirst for righteousness,
for they will be filled.
MATTHEW 5:6 NIV

Because you are an imperfect human being, you are not "perfectly" happy—and that's perfectly okay with God. He is far less concerned with your happiness than He is with your holiness.

God continuously reveals Himself in everyday life, but He does not do so in order to make you contented; He does so in order to lead you to His Son. So don't be overly concerned with your current level of happiness; it will change. Be more concerned with the current state of your relationship with Christ: He does not change. And because your Savior transcends time and space, you can be comforted in the knowledge that in the end, His joy will become your joy . . . for all eternity.

2 minutes A DAY

more stuff to think about

In heaven, we will see that nothing, absolutely nothing, was
wasted, and that every tear counted
and every cry was heard.

JONI EARECKSON TADA

Our ultimate aim in life is not to be healthy,
wealthy, prosperous, or problem free.
Our ultimate aim in life is to bring glory to God.

ANNE GRAHAM LOTZ

Holiness isn't in a style of dress. It's not a matter of rules
and regulations. It's a way of life that emanates quietness
and rest, joy in family, shared pleasures with friends,
the help of a neighbor—and the hope of a Savior.

JONI EARECKSON TADA

The Big Idea

God is holy and wants you to be holy. Christ died to make
you holy. Make sure that your response to Christ's sacrifice is
worthy of Him.

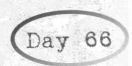

He's Waiting at the Door

Ask, and God will give to you. Search, and you will find.
Knock, and the door will open for you. Yes, everyone who
asks will receive. Everyone who searches will find.
And everyone who knocks will have the door opened.

MATTHEW 7:7-8 NCV

Is God hanging out at the far end of the universe, too far away to hear your requests? Nope, God is right here, right now, waiting to hear from you. Are you ready to talk to Him? Hopefully, you've learned the wisdom of asking God for His help.

Are you in need? Ask God to sustain you. Are you troubled? Take your worries to Him, and He will comfort you. Are you weary? Seek God's strength. Do you have questions about your future that you simply can't answer? Ask your Heavenly Father for insight and direction. In all things great and small, seek God's wisdom and His will. He will hear your prayers, and He will answer.

more stuff to think about

Through the death and broken body of Jesus Christ
on the Cross, you and I have been given access to the
presence of God when we approach Him by faith in prayer.

ANNE GRAHAM LOTZ

If you want to hear God's voice clearly and you are
uncertain, then remain in His presence until He changes that
uncertainty. Often, much can happen during this waiting for
the Lord. Sometimes, he changes pride into humility,
doubt into faith and peace.

CORRIE TEN BOOM

The Big Idea

If you want more from life, ask more from God: D. L. Moody
observed, "Some people think God does not like to be
troubled with our constant asking. But, the way to trouble
God is not to come at all." So, if you want to know God
better—or if you seek any other worthy goal—ask Him (and
keep asking Him) until He answers your prayers.

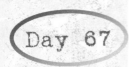

Keep Growing

*As newborn babies want milk, you should want
the pure and simple teaching.
By it you can grow up and be saved.*

1 PETER 2:2 NCV

If you sincerely want to know God, then you can't be
satisfied to be a stagnant believer.

God's plan for you includes a lifetime of prayer, praise,
and spiritual growth. As a Christian, you can—and should—
continue to grow in the love and the knowledge of your
Savior as long as you live.

If you cease to grow, either emotionally or spiritually, you
do yourself a profound disservice. But, if you study God's
Word, if you obey His commandments, and if you live in the
protection of His will, you will not be a stagnant believer;
you will, instead, be a growing Christian . . . and that's
exactly what God wants you to be.

2 minutes a day

more stuff to think about

God loves us the way we are,
but He loves us too much to leave us that way.

LEIGHTON FORD

Look upon chastening as God's chariots sent to carry
your soul into the high places of spiritual achievement.

HANNAH WHITALL SMITH

You are either becoming more like Christ every day or
you're becoming less like Him.
There is no neutral position in the Lord.

STORMIE OMARTIAN

The Big Idea

Growing to spiritual maturity requires a plan. What is yours?

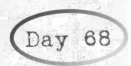
Don't Fall Prey to Envy

*We can't afford to waste a minute, must not squander
these precious daylight hours in frivolity and indulgence, in
sleeping around and dissipation, in bickering and grabbing
everything in sight. Get out of bed and get dressed!
Don't loiter and linger, waiting until the very last minute.
Dress yourselves in Christ, and be up and about!*

ROMANS 13:13-14 MSG

Because we are imperfect, we are sometimes envious of
others. But to be envious is to be foolish. So we must
guard ourselves against the natural tendency to feel
resentment and jealousy when other people experience good
fortune. Rather than succumbing to feelings of envy, we
should focus on the marvelous things that God has done for
us (and we should refrain from preoccupying ourselves with
the blessings that God has chosen to give others).

St. John Chrysostom offered these words of caution:
"As a moth gnaws a garment, so does envy consume a
man." So here's a proven formula for a happier, healthier
life: Count your own blessings and let your neighbors count
theirs. It's the best way to live.

more stuff to think about

Contentment comes when we develop an attitude of gratitude for the important things we do have in our lives that we tend to take for granted if we have our eyes staring longingly at our neighbor's stuff.

DAVE RAMSEY

What God asks, does, or requires of others is not my business; it is His.

KAY ARTHUR

When you envy your neighbor, you give demons a place to rest.

EPHRAEM THE SYRIAN

The Big Idea

Feelings of envy will rob you of happiness and peace. Don't allow yourself to be robbed.

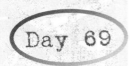

Contagious Christianity

*All those who stand before others
and say they believe in me, I will say before my Father
in heaven that they belong to me.*

MATTHEW 10:32 NCV

Genuine, heartfelt Christianity is contagious. If you enjoy a life-altering relationship with God, that relationship will inevitably have an impact on others—perhaps a profound impact.

Are you excited about your growing relationship with God—and do you make your enthusiasm known to those around you? Or are you a "silent ambassador" for Christ? God's preference is clear: He intends that you stand before others and proclaim your faith. So share your testimony and your excitement. The world needs both.

more stuff to think about

The people whom I have seen succeed best in life have always been cheerful and hopeful people who went about their business with a smile on their faces.

CHARLES KINGSLEY

Sour godliness is the devil's religion.

JOHN WESLEY

In their heart of hearts, I think all true followers of Christ long to become contagious Christians. Though unsure about how to do so or the risks involved, deep down they sense that there isn't anything as rewarding as opening a person up to God's love and truth.

BILL HYBELS

The Big Idea

If you want to be a faithful follower of Jesus . . . follow in His footsteps every day, obey His commandments every day, and share His never-ending love—every day.

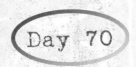

Be Silent

Be silent before the LORD and wait expectantly for Him.
PSALM 37:7 HOLMAN CSB

Sometimes God speaks loudly and clearly. More often, He speaks in a quiet voice—and if you are wise, you will be listening carefully when He does. To do so, you must carve out quiet moments each day to study His Word and sense His direction.

Can you quiet yourself long enough to listen to your conscience? Are you attuned to the subtle guidance of your intuition? Are you willing to pray sincerely and then to wait quietly for God's response. Hopefully so. Usually God refrains from sending His messages on stone tablets or city billboards. More often, He communicates in subtler ways. If you sincerely desire to hear His voice, you must listen carefully, and you must do so in the silent corners of your quiet, willing heart.

2 minutes A DAY

more stuff to think about

Most of man's trouble comes from his inability to be still.

BLAISE PASCAL

When an honest soul can get still before the living Christ,
we can still hear Him say simply and clearly,
"Love the Lord your God with all your heart and with
all your soul and with all your mind . . .
and love one another as I have loved you."

GLORIA GAITHER

Be still, and in the quiet moments, listen to the voice of
your heavenly Father. His words can renew your spirit.
No one knows you and your needs like He does.

JANET L. WEAVER

The Big Idea

Try this experiment: the next time you're driving alone in your
automobile, do so without radio, CDs, or cell phones. And
then, have a quiet talk with God about His plans for your
life. You may be surprised to discover that sometimes the
most important answers are the ones you receive in silence.

When the Path Is Dark

Though I sit in darkness, the LORD will be my light.
MICAH 7:8 HOLMAN CSB

Doubts come in several shapes and sizes: doubts about God, doubts about the future, and doubts about our own abilities, for starters. But when doubts creep in, as they will from time to time, we need not despair. As Sheila Walsh observed, "To wrestle with God does not mean that we have lost faith, but that we are fighting for it."

God never leaves our side, not for an instant. He is always with us, always willing to calm the storms of life. When we sincerely seek His presence—and when we genuinely seek to establish a deeper, more meaningful relationship with Him—God is prepared to touch our hearts, to calm our fears, to answer our doubts, and to restore our confidence.

2 minutes A DAY

more stuff to think about

Doubting may temporarily disturb,
but will not permanently destroy, your faith in Christ.

CHARLES SWINDOLL

In heaven, we will see that nothing, absolutely nothing, was
wasted, and that every tear counted
and every cry was heard.

JONI EARECKSON TADA

Feelings of uselessness and hopelessness are not from God,
but from the evil one, the devil, who wants to discourage
you and thwart your effectiveness for the Lord.

BILL BRIGHT

The Big Idea

Difficult days come and go. Stay the course. The sun is
shining somewhere, and will soon shine on you.

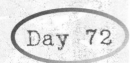

Don't Fall in Love with Money

For where your treasure is, there your heart will be also.
LUKE 12:34 NKJV

Our society is in love with money and the things that money can buy. God is not. God cares about people, not possessions, and so must we.

Even though we live in a world that seems to worship stuff, we must not allow ourselves to fall in love with our possessions. We must, instead, try to focus more on the things that are important to God (and less upon the things that are important to society).

Money, in and of itself, is not evil; worshipping money is. So today, as you seek better ways to know your Creator, remember that God is almighty, but the dollar is not.

more stuff to think about

The Scriptures also reveal warnings that if we are consumed with greed, not only do we disobey God, but we will miss the opportunity to allow Him to use us as instruments for others.

CHARLES STANLEY

Money is a mirror that, strange as it sounds, reflects our personal weaknesses and strengths with amazing clarity.

DAVE RAMSEY

God is entitled to a portion of our income. Not because he needs it, but because we need to give it.

JAMES DOBSON

The Big Idea

A greedy lifestyle is never fulfilling because greed leads to a constant (and unsuccessful) attempt to find happiness and abundance apart from God.

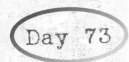

Worry Less

*Do not worry about anything, but pray and ask God for
everything you need, always giving thanks.*
PHILIPPIANS 4:6 NCV

When we're worried, there are two places we should
take our concerns: to the people who love us and
to God.

When troubles arise, it helps to talk about them with
parents, concerned adults, and trusted friends. But we
shouldn't stop there: we should also talk to God through our
prayers.

If you're worried about something, pray about it.
Remember that God is always listening, and He always
wants to hear from you.

So when you're upset, try this simple plan: talk and pray.
Talk openly to the people who love you, and pray to the
Heavenly Father who made you. The more you talk and the
more you pray, the better you'll feel.

2 minutes a day

more stuff to think about

Refuse to be swamped by the cares of the world.

OSWALD CHAMBERS

Anxiety is not only a pain which we must ask God to assuage
but also a weakness we must ask him to pardon—
for he's told us to take no care for the morrow.

C. S. LEWIS

Walk by faith! Stop the plague of worry.
Relax! Learn to say, "Lord, this is Your battle."

CHARLES SWINDOLL

The Big Idea

I believe that it is important to try to live in "day-tight"
compartments by not fretting too much about yesterday or
tomorrow.

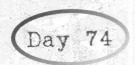

Walking in the Light

I am the light of the world. Whoever follows me will never walk in darkness, but will have the light of life.

JOHN 8:12 NIV

God's Holy Word instructs us that Jesus is, "the way, the truth, and the life" (John 14:6-7). Without Christ, we are as far removed from salvation as the east is removed from the west. And without Christ, we can never know the ultimate truth: God's truth.

Truth is God's way: He commands His believers to live in truth, and He rewards those who do so. Jesus is the personification of God's liberating truth, a truth that offers salvation to mankind.

Do you seek to walk with God? Do you seek to feel His presence and His peace? Then you must walk in truth; you must walk in the light; you must walk with the Savior. There is simply no other way.

2 minutes A DAY

more stuff to think about

Our battles are first won or lost in the secret places of
our will in God's presence, never in full view of the world.

OSWALD CHAMBERS

The Christian faith is meant to be lived moment by moment.
It isn't some broad, general outline—it's a long walk with
a real Person. Details count: passing thoughts,
small sacrifices, a few encouraging words,
little acts of kindness, brief victories over nagging sins.

JONI EARECKSON TADA

Jesus differs from all other teachers; they reach the ear,
but he instructs the heart; they deal with the outward letter,
but he imparts an inward taste for the truth.

C. H. SPURGEON

The Big Idea

Let your light shine: The way that you behave yourself is like
a light that shines out upon the world. Make sure that your
light is both bright and good.

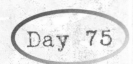

Forgive Everybody

In prayer there is a connection between what God does and what you do. You can't get forgiveness from God, for instance, without also forgiving others. If you refuse to do your part, you cut yourself off from God's part.

MATTHEW 6:14-15 MSG

Are you the kind of person who has a tough time forgiving and forgetting? If so, welcome to the club. Plenty of people find that it's difficult to forgive—difficult, but not impossible.

Life would be much simpler if you could forgive other people "once and for all" and be done with it. Yet forgiveness is seldom that easy. Usually, the decision to forgive is straightforward, but the process of forgiving is more difficult. Forgiveness is a journey that requires effort, time, perseverance, and prayer.

If there exists even one person whom you have not forgiven (and that includes the person you see when you look in the mirror), obey God's commandment: forgive that person today. And while you're at it, remember this: bitterness, anger, and regret are not part of God's plan for your life. Forgiveness is.

more stuff to think about

I believe that forgiveness can become a continuing cycle:
because God forgives us, we're to forgive others;
because we forgive others, God forgives us.
Scripture presents both parts of the cycle.

SHIRLEY DOBSON

Only the truly forgiven are truly forgiving.

C. S. LEWIS

Learning how to forgive and forget is one of the secrets
of a happy Christian life.

WARREN WIERSBE

The Big Idea

If you're having trouble forgiving someone else . . . think
how many times other people have forgiven you!

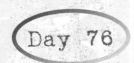

Seek Strength from God

The LORD is my strength and my song; he has become
my victory. He is my God, and I will praise him.
EXODUS 15:2 NLT

Where do you go to find strength? The gym? The health food store? The espresso bar? There's a better source of strength, of course, and that source is God. He is a never-ending source of strength and courage if you call upon Him.

Have you "tapped in" to the power of God? Have you turned your life and your heart over to Him, or are you muddling along under your own power? The answer to this question will determine the quality of your life here on earth and the destiny of your life throughout all eternity. So start tapping in—and remember that when it comes to strength, God is the Ultimate Source.

2 MINUTES A DAY

more stuff to think about

Hope can give us life. It can provide energy that would
otherwise do us in completely if we tried to operate
in our own strength.

BARBARA JOHNSON

Sometimes I think spiritual and physical strength is like
manna: you get just what you need for the day, no more.

SUZANNE DALE EZELL

All the power of God—the same power that hung the stars
in place and put the planets in their courses and transformed
Earth—now resides in you to energize and strengthen you
to become the person God created you to be.

ANNE GRAHAM LOTZ

The Big Idea

Need strength? Slow down, get more rest, engage in
sensible exercise, and turn your troubles over to God . . . .
but not necessarily in that order.

Be Humble

*Humble yourselves, therefore, under God's mighty hand,
that he may lift you up in due time.*

1 PETER 5:6 NIV

O n the road to spiritual growth, pride is a massive
roadblock. The more prideful you are, the more
difficult it is to know God. When you experience
success, it's easy to puff out your chest and proclaim, "I did
that!" Easy, but wrong.

Dietrich Bonhoeffer observed, "It is very easy to
overestimate the importance of our own achievements," and
he was right.

So, the next time you're tempted to take too much credit
for something you've done, resist the temptation. Instead of
hogging all the glory, give God His fair share of the credit . . .
and His share, by the way, is far bigger than your share.

more stuff to think about

Do you wish to rise? Begin by descending.
You plan a tower that will pierce the clouds?
Lay first the foundation of humility.

ST. AUGUSTINE

We can never have more of true faith
than we have of true humility.

ANDREW MURRAY

Nothing sets a person so much out of
the devil's reach as humility.

JONATHAN EDWARDS

The Big Idea

Do you value humility above status? If so, God will smile
upon your endeavors. But if you value status above humility,
you're inviting God's displeasure. In short, humility pleases
God; pride does not.

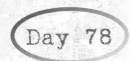

Be a Practical Christian

Pure and lasting religion in the sight of God our Father means that we must care for orphans and widows in their troubles, and refuse to let the world corrupt us.

JAMES 1:27 NLT

As Christians, we must do our best to ensure that our actions are accurate reflections of our beliefs. Our theology must be demonstrated, not only by our words but, more importantly, by our actions. In short, we should be practical believers, quick to act whenever we see an opportunity to serve God.

Are you the kind of practical Christian who is willing to dig in and do what needs to be done when it needs to be done? If so, congratulations: God acknowledges your service and blesses it. But if you find yourself more interested in the fine points of theology than in the needs of your neighbors, it's time to rearrange your priorities. God needs believers who are willing to roll up their sleeves and go to work for Him. Count yourself among that number. Theology is a good thing unless it interferes with God's work. And it's up to you to make certain that your theology doesn't.

more stuff to think about

Had Jesus been the Word become word,
He would have spun theories about life,
but since he was the Word become flesh,
he put shoes on all his theories and made them walk.

E. STANLEY JONES

But the proper aim of giving is to put the recipient in
a state where he no longer needs our gift.

C. S. LEWIS

Practice amongst yourselves charity, charity, charity . . .
and zeal for the salvation of souls.

ST. EUGENE DE MAZENOD

The Big Idea

Not just on Sunday! . . . Do something every day that helps
another person have a better life.

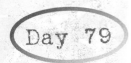

Day 79

Be Patient and Trust God

Trust in him at all times, O people;
pour out your hearts to him, for God is our refuge.

PSALM 62:8 NIV

We are impatient for the changes we so earnestly desire. We want solutions to our problems, and we want them right now! But sometimes, life's greatest challenges defy easy solutions, so we must be patient.

Psalm 37:7 commands us to "Rest in the LORD, and wait patiently for Him" (NKJV). But for most of us, waiting quietly for God is difficult. Why? Because we are imperfect beings who seek solutions to our problems today, if not sooner. We seek to manage our lives according to our own timetables, not God's. To do so is a mistake.

Instead of impatiently tapping our fingers, we should fold our fingers and pray. When we do, our Heavenly Father will reward us in His own miraculous way and in His own perfect time.

2 minutes A DAY

more stuff to think about

Be patient. God is using today's difficulties to strengthen
you for tomorrow. He is equipping you.
The God who makes things grow will help you bear fruit.

MAX LUCADO

We must never think that patience is complacency.
Patience is endurance in action.

WARREN WIERSBE

God freely admits he is holding back his power,
but he restrains himself for our benefit. For all scoffers
who call for direct action from the heavens, the prophets
have ominous advice: Just wait.

PHILIP YANCEY

The Big Idea

You have a timetable, and God has a timetable. His is better
than yours.

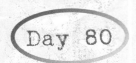

Disciplined?

So prepare your minds for service and have self-control.
All your hope should be for the gift of grace that will be
yours when Jesus Christ is shown to you.

1 PETER 1:13 NCV

Sometimes, it's hard to be dignified and disciplined. Why? Because you live in a world where many prominent people want you to believe that dignified, self-disciplined behavior is going out of style. But don't kid yourself: self-discipline never goes out of style.

Face facts: Life's greatest rewards aren't likely to fall into your lap. On the contrary, your greatest accomplishments will probably require plenty of work and a heaping helping of self-discipline—which, by the way, is perfectly fine with God. After all, He knows that you're up to the task, and He has big plans for you. God will do His part to fulfill those plans, and the rest, of course, depends upon you.

2 MINUTES A DAY

more stuff to think about

True willpower and courage are not on the battlefield,
but in everyday conquests over our inertia,
laziness, and boredom.

D. L. MOODY

Work is doing it. Discipline is doing it every day.
Diligence is doing it well every day.

DAVE RAMSEY

If one examines the secret behind a championship football
team, a magnificent orchestra, or a successful business,
the principal ingredient is invariably discipline.

JAMES DOBSON

The Big Idea

First you make choices . . . and pretty soon those choices
begin to shape your life. That's why you must make smart
choices . . . or face the consequences of making dumb
ones.

The Right Kind of Peer Pressure

As iron sharpens iron, so people can improve each other.
PROVERBS 27:17 NCV

Because we tend to become like our friends, we must choose our friends carefully. Because our friends influence us in ways that are both subtle and powerful, we must ensure that our friendships are pleasing to God. When we spend our days in the presence of godly believers, we are blessed, not only by those friends, but also by our Creator.

Are you hanging out with people who make you a better Christian, or are you spending time with people who encourage you to stray from your faith? The answer to this question will have a surprising impact on the condition of your spiritual health. Why? Because peer pressure is very real and very powerful. So, one of the best ways to ensure that you follow Christ is to find fellow believers who are willing to follow Him with you.

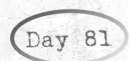
2 minutes a day

more stuff to think about

If you choose to awaken a passion for God,
you will have to choose your friends wisely.

LISA BEVERE

The effective mentor strives to help a man or woman
discover what they can be in Christ and then holds them
accountable to become that person.

HOWARD HENDRICKS

We urgently need people who encourage and
inspire us to move toward God and away from
the world's enticing pleasures.

JIM CYMBALA

The Big Idea

Put peer pressure to work for you. How? By associating with
people who, by their actions and their words, will encourage
you to become a better person.

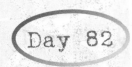

Be a Cheerful Christian

The cheerful heart has a continual feast.
PROVERBS 15:15 NIV

Few things in life are more sad, or, for that matter, more absurd, than a grumpy Christian. Christ promises us lives of abundance and joy, but He does not force His joy upon us. We must claim His joy for ourselves, and when we do, Jesus, in turn, fills our spirits with His power and His love.

How can we receive from Christ the joy that is rightfully ours? By giving Him what is rightfully His: our hearts and our souls.

When we earnestly commit ourselves to the Savior of mankind, when we place Jesus at the center of our lives and trust Him as our personal Savior, He will transform us, not just for today, but for all eternity. Then we, as God's children, can share Christ's joy and His message with a world that needs both.

2 minutes A DAY

more stuff to think about

Be merry, really merry. The life of a true Christian should be
a perpetual jubilee, a prelude to the festivals of eternity.

THEOPHARE VENARD

Christ can put a spring in your step and a thrill in your heart.
Optimism and cheerfulness are products of knowing Christ.

BILLY GRAHAM

The greatest honor you can give Almighty God
is to live gladly and joyfully because of the
knowledge of His love.

JULIANA OF NORWICH

The Big Idea

Do you need a little cheering up? Cheer up somebody else.
When you brighten somebody else's day, you brighten up
your own day, too.

Thankful?

*And those who have reason to be thankful should
continually sing praises to the Lord.*
JAMES 5:13 NLT

God's Word makes it clear: a wise heart is a thankful heart. Period. Your Heavenly Father has blessed you beyond measure, and you owe Him everything, including your thanks.

If you are a thoughtful Christian, you will be a thankful Christian. No matter your circumstances, you owe God so much more than you can ever repay, and you owe Him your heartfelt thanks. So thank Him . . . and keep thanking Him, today, tomorrow and forever. God is always listening—are you willing to say thanks? It's up to you, and the next move is always yours.

more stuff to think about

The game was to just find something about everything
to be glad about—no matter what it was.
You see, when you're hunting for the glad things,
you sort of forget the other kind.

ELEANOR H. PORTER

It is only with gratitude that life becomes rich.

DIETRICH BONHOEFFER

Thank God every morning when you get up that you have
something to do that day which must be done,
whether you like it or not.

CHARLES KINGSLEY

The Big Idea

When is the best time to say "thanks" to God? Any time.
God never takes a vacation, and He's always ready to hear
from you. So what are you waiting for?

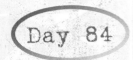

Follow Him

Whoever serves me must follow me.
Then my servant will be with me everywhere I am.
My Father will honor anyone who serves me.

JOHN 12:26 NCV

Whom will you walk with today? Will you walk with people who worship the ways of the world? Or will you walk with the Son of God?

Jesus walks with you. Are you walking with Him? Hopefully, you will choose to walk with Him today and every day of your life.

Jesus has called upon believers of every generation (and that includes you) to follow in His footsteps. And God's Word promises that when you follow in Christ's footsteps, you will learn how to live freely and lightly (Matthew 11:28-30).

Are you worried about the day ahead? Be confident in God's power. He will never desert you. Are you concerned about the future? Be courageous and call upon God. He will protect you. Are you confused? Listen to the quiet voice of your Heavenly Father. He is not a God of confusion. Talk with God; listen to Him; follow His commandments . . . and walk with His Son—starting now.

more stuff to think about

A heart out of tune, out of sync with God's heart, will
produce a life of spiritual barrenness
and missed opportunities.

JIM CYMBALA

Peter said, "No, Lord!" But he had to learn that
one cannot say "No" while saying "Lord"
and that one cannot say "Lord" while saying "No."

CORRIE TEN BOOM

As you pause to consider the kind of Christian you are—
and the kind of Christian you want to become—ask yourself
whether you're standing in the light or sitting on the fence.

CRISWELL FREEMAN

The Big Idea

Following Christ is a matter of obedience. If you want to be
a little more like Jesus . . . learn about His teachings, follow
in His footsteps, and obey His commandments.

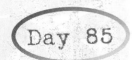

Don't Get Tired of Doing the Right Thing

Let us not become weary in doing good, for at the proper time we will reap a harvest if we do not give up.

GALATIANS 6:9 NIV

The world you live in has a way of testing your faith, your courage, and your intentions. If you intend to follow God (and if you follow through on those intentions) you'll be rewarded . . . richly rewarded. But if you cave in at the first temptation, you're headed for trouble, and fast.

Whose steps will you follow today? Will you honor God as you strive to follow His Son? Or will you join the lockstep legion that seeks to discover happiness and fulfillment through worldly means? If you are righteous and wise, you will follow Christ. You will follow Him today and every day. You will seek to walk in His footsteps without reservation or doubt. When you do so, you will be "right with God" precisely because you are walking with His only begotten Son.

2 minutes a day

more stuff to think about

Don't worry about what you do not understand.
Worry about what you do understand in the Bible
but do not live by.

CORRIE TEN BOOM

No more duty can be urged upon those who are
entering the great theater of life than simple loyalty
to their best convictions.

EDWIN HUBBEL CHAPIN

In the fulfillment of your duties, let your intentions be
so pure that you reject from your actions any other
motive than the glory of God and the salvation of souls.

ANGELA MERICI

The Big Idea

Today, consider the value of living a life that is pleasing to
God. And while you're at it, think about the rewards that are
likely to be yours when you do the right thing day in and day
out.

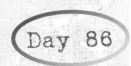

Jesus Was a Servant (And You Must Be, Too)

Be strong and of good courage, and do it; do not fear nor be dismayed, for the LORD God—my God—will be with you. He will not leave you nor forsake you, until you have finished all the work for the service of the house of the LORD.

1 CHRONICLES 28:20 NKJV

If you want to know God, you should do your best to imitate His Son. How? One way you can do it is by being a humble servant, just like Jesus was.

You live in a world that glorifies power, prestige, fame, and money. But the words of Jesus teach us that the most esteemed men and women are not the widely acclaimed leaders of society; the most esteemed among us are the humble servants of society.

So here's your choice: you can serve yourself (and follow the ways of the world) or you can serve your friends and neighbors (and follow Jesus). If you really want to know the Father and the Son, you must choose the latter.

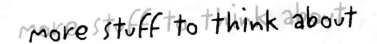
more stuff to think about

Carve your name on hearts, not on marble.

C. H. SPURGEON

There are times when we are called to love, expecting
nothing in return. There are times when we are called to give
money to people who will never say thanks, to forgive those
who won't forgive us, to come early and stay late
when no one else notices.

MAX LUCADO

I have discovered that when I please Christ,
I end up inadvertently serving others far more effectively.

BETH MOORE

The Big Idea

Whatever your age, whatever your circumstances, you can
serve: Each stage of life's journey is a glorious opportunity to
place yourself in the service of the One who is the Giver of
all blessings. As long as you live, you should honor God with
your service to others.

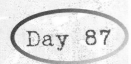

Share Your Testimony

This and this only has been my appointed work:
getting this news to those who have never heard of God,
and explaining how it works by simple faith and plain truth.
1 Timothy 2:7 MSG

A good way to build your faith is by talking about it—and that's precisely what God wants you to do. Let's face facts: You live in a world that desperately needs the healing message of Jesus Christ. Every believer, including you, bears responsibility for sharing the Good News. And it is important to remember that you give your testimony through your words and your actions.

As your faith becomes stronger, you will find ways to share your beliefs with your family, with your friends, with your dates, and with the world. And when you do, everybody wins.

more stuff to think about

Being an effective witness means that we call attention to
our testimony and leave the results to Him.

CALVIN MILLER

No matter how crazy or nutty your life has seemed,
God can make something strong and good out of it.
He can help you grow wide branches for others
to use as shelter.

BARBARA JOHNSON

But what hope have we if, while singing "Onward Christian
Soldiers," we go through perfunctory services, parroting
prayers, yawning over watches, acting as if we were
excursionists on a pleasure expedition?

R. G. LEE

The Big Idea

If your eternity with God is secure (because you believe in
Jesus), you have a profound responsibility to tell as many
people as you can about the eternal life that Christ offers to
those who believe in Him.

Open Yourself Up to God's Surprising Plans

But as it is written: What no eye has seen and no ear has heard, and what has never come into a man's heart, is what God has prepared for those who love Him.

1 CORINTHIANS 2:9 HOLMAN CSB

God has plans for your life, wonderful, surprising plans . . . but He won't force those plans upon you. To the contrary, He has given you free will, the ability to make decisions on your own. With that freedom to choose comes the responsibility of living with the consequences of the choices you make.

If you seek to live in accordance with God's will for your life—and you should—then you will live in accordance with His commandments. You will study God's Word, and you will be watchful for His signs. You will associate with fellow Christians who will encourage your spiritual growth, and you will listen to that inner voice that speaks to you in the quiet moments of your daily devotionals.

God intends to use you in wonderful, unexpected ways if you let Him. The decision to seek God's plan and to follow it is yours and yours alone. The consequences of that decision have implications that are both profound and eternal, so choose carefully.

2 MINUTES A DAY

more stuff to think about

Joy is what happens to us when we allow ourselves to recognize how good things really are.

MARIANNE WILLIAMSON

God surrounds you with opportunity. You and I are free in Jesus Christ, not to do whatever we want, but to be all that God wants us to be.

WARREN WIERSBE

Even when we cannot see the why and wherefore of God's dealings, we know that there is love in and behind them, so we can rejoice always.

J. I. PACKER

The Big Idea

God has a wonderful plan for your life. And the time to start looking for that plan—and living it—is now. And remember—discovering God's plan begins with prayer.

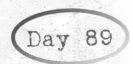

When You Just Don't Understand

Now we see a dim reflection, as if we were looking into a mirror, but then we shall see clearly. Now I know only a part, but then I will know fully, as God has known me.

1 CORINTHIANS 13:12 NCV

As humans with limited understanding, we can never fully comprehend the hand of God. But as believers in a benevolent God, we must always trust the heart of our Heavenly Father.

Before His crucifixion, Jesus went to the Mount of Olives and poured out His heart to God (Luke 22). Jesus knew of the agony that He was destined to endure, but He also knew that God's will must be done. We, like our Savior, face trials that bring fear and trembling to the very depths of our souls, but like Christ, we, too, must ultimately seek God's will, not our own.

As this day unfolds, seek God's will for your own life and obey His Word. When you entrust your life to Him completely and without reservation, He will give you the strength to meet any challenge, the courage to face any trial, and the wisdom to live in His righteousness and in His peace.

more stuff to think about

In perplexities—when we cannot tell what to do,
when we cannot understand what is going on around us—
let us be calmed and steadied and made patient by
the thought that what is hidden from us is not
hidden from Him.

FRANCES RIDLEY HAVERGAL

Where there is no longer any opportunity for doubt,
there is no longer any opportunity for faith, either.

PAUL TOURNIER

A religion that is small enough for our understanding
would not be big enough for our needs.

CORRIE TEN BOOM

The Big Idea

Don't spend too much time asking, "Why me, Lord?"
Instead, ask, "What now, Lord?" and then get to work. When
you do, you'll feel much better.

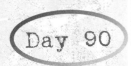

Let God Guide the Way

*The true children of God are those who
let God's Spirit lead them.*
ROMANS 8:14 NCV

The Bible promises that God will guide you if you let Him. Your job is to let Him. But sometimes, you will be tempted to do otherwise. Sometimes, you'll be tempted to go along with the crowd; other times, you'll be tempted to do things your way, not God's way. When you feel these temptations, resist them.

God has promised that when you ask for His help, He will not withhold it. So ask. Ask Him to meet the needs of your day. Ask Him to lead you, to protect you, and to correct you. And trust the answers He gives.

God stands at the door and waits. When you knock, He opens. When you ask, He answers. Your task, of course, is to seek His guidance prayerfully, confidently, and often.

more stuff to think about

Only He can guide you to invest your life in worthwhile ways.
This guidance will come as you "walk"
with Him and listen to Him.

HENRY BLACKABY AND CLAUDE KING

Is God your spare wheel or your steering wheel?

ANONYMOUS

Are you serious about wanting God's guidance to become
a personal reality in your life? The first step is to tell
God that you know you can't manage your own life;
that you need his help.

CATHERINE MARSHALL

The Big Idea

Pray for guidance. When you ask for it, He will give it.

Make God the Cornerstone

*For the eyes of the Lord are on the righteous
and his ears are attentive to their prayer,
but the Lord is against those who do evil.*

1 PETER 3:12 NIV

Have you made God the cornerstone of your life, or is He relegated to a few hours on Sunday morning? Have you genuinely allowed God to reign over every corner of your heart, or have you attempted to place Him in a spiritual compartment? The answer to these questions will determine the direction of your day and your life.

God loves you. In times of trouble, He will comfort you; in times of sorrow, He will dry your tears. When you are weak or sorrowful, God is as near as your next breath. He stands at the door of your heart and waits. Welcome Him in and allow Him to rule. And then, accept the peace and the strength and the protection and the abundance that only God can give.

more stuff to think about

Whatever you love most, be it sports, pleasure, business, or God, that is your god.

BILLY GRAHAM

If choosing to spend time alone with God is a real struggle—a heavy-handed demand that only adds more guilt and stress to your already overblown schedule—it's time to change the way you approach his presence.

DORIS GREIG

God can do all that we need.

JULIANA OF NORWICH

The Big Idea

Today, think about . . . ways that you can glorify God by placing Him first in your life.

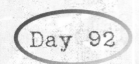

Make Christ Your Focus

*I do not consider myself yet to have taken hold of it.
But one thing I do: Forgetting what is behind and straining
toward what is ahead, I press on toward the goal
to win the prize for which God has called me
heavenward in Christ Jesus.*

PHILIPPIANS 3:13-14 NIV

Is Christ the focus of your life? Are you fired with enthusiasm for Him? Are you an energized Christian who allows God's Son to reign over every aspect of your day? Make no mistake: that's exactly what God intends for you to do.

God has given you the gift of eternal life through His Son. In response to God's priceless gift, you are instructed to focus your thoughts, your prayers, and your energies upon God and His only begotten Son. To do so, you must resist the subtle yet powerful temptation to become a "spiritual dabbler."

A person who dabbles in the Christian faith is unwilling to place God in His rightful place: above all other things. Resist that temptation; make God the cornerstone and the touchstone of your life. When you do, He will give you all the strength and wisdom you need to live victoriously for Him.

2 MINUTES A DAY

more stuff to think about

Whatever is your best time in the day, give that to communion with God.

HUDSON TAYLOR

I don't see how any Christian can survive,
let alone live life as more than a conqueror,
apart from a quiet time alone with God.

KAY ARTHUR

Give me the person who says,
"This one thing I do, and not these fifty things I dabble in."

D. L. MOODY

The Big Idea

Jesus made an amazing sacrifice for you . . . what kind of
sacrifice are you willing to make for Him?

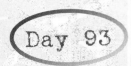

Read the Bible Every Day

Your word is a lamp to my feet and a light for my path.
PSALM 119:105 NIV

If you're serious about really getting to know God better, then you'll need to get really serious about reading your Bible every day (not just on Sundays!).

The Bible is unlike any other book. It is a priceless gift from your Creator, a tool that God intends for you to use in every aspect of your life. And, it contains promises upon which you, as a Christian, can and must depend.

D. L. Moody observed, "The Bible was not given to increase our knowledge but to change our lives." God's Holy Word is, indeed, a life-changing, one-of-a-kind treasure. Handle it with care, but more importantly, handle it every day.

more stuff to think about

The Lord Jesus, available to people much of the time,
left them, sometimes a great while before day,
to go up to the hills where He could commune
in solitude with His Father.

ELISABETH ELLIOT

Quiet time is giving God your undivided attention for
a predetermined amount of time for the purpose
of talking to and hearing from Him.

CHARLES STANLEY

Jesus taught us by example to get out of the rat race
and recharge our batteries.

BARBARA JOHNSON

The Big Idea

If you have a choice to make, the Bible can help you make
it. If you've got questions, the Bible has answers.

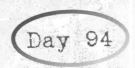

Give God the Glory

*Respect for the Lord will teach you wisdom.
If you want to be honored, you must be humble.*
PROVERBS 15:33 NCV

Who are the greatest among us? Are they the proud and the powerful? Hardly. The greatest among us are the humble servants who care less for their own glory and more for God's glory. So, if you seek greatness in God's eyes, you must forever praise God's good works, not your own.

If you're tempted to overestimate your own accomplishments, resist that temptation. Instead of puffing out your chest and saying, "Look at me!" give credit where credit is due, starting with God. And, rest assured: There is no such thing as a "self-made" man (or woman). All of us are made by God . . . and He deserves the glory, not us.

more stuff to think about

Faithful prayer warriors and devoted Bible lovers will tell you
that their passion for disciplined quiet time with the Lord is
not a sign of strength but an admission of weakness—
a hard-earned realization that they are nothing on their own
compared with who they are after they've been with him.

DORIS GREIG

O soul, only He who created you can satisfy you.
If you ask for anything else, it is your misfortune.

ST. AUGUSTINE

O Lord our God, grant us grace to desire thee with our
whole heart; so that desiring, we may seek, and seeking,
find thee; and so finding thee, and loving thee,
may hate those sins from which thou hast redeemed us.

ST. ANSELM OF CANTERBURY

The Big Idea

Thoughtful believers (like you) make it a habit to carve out
quiet moments throughout the day to praise God.

Trust the Future to God

*"I say this because I know what I am planning for you,"
says the Lord. "I have good plans for you, not plans
to hurt you. I will give you hope and a good future."*
JEREMIAH 29:11 NCV

How can you get to know God if you're unwilling to trust Him? The answer, of course, is that you can't. That's why you should trust God in everything (and that means entrusting your future to God).

Do you trust in the ultimate goodness of God's plan for your life? Will you face tomorrow's challenges with optimism and hope? You should. After all, God created you for a very important reason: His reason. And you still have important work to do: His work.

Today, as you live in the present and look to the future, remember that God has an amazing plan for you. Act—and believe—accordingly.

more stuff to think about

Our future may look fearfully intimidating,
yet we can look up to the Engineer of the Universe,
confident that nothing escapes His attention or slips out of
the control of those strong hands.

ELISABETH ELLIOT

Never be afraid to trust an unknown future to a known God.

CORRIE TEN BOOM

Allow your dreams a place in your prayers and plans.
God-given dreams can help you move into the future
He is preparing for you.

BARBARA JOHNSON

The Big Idea

The future isn't some pie-in-the-sky dream. Hope for the
future is simply one aspect of trusting God.

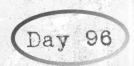

What to Do About Evil

Take your stand with God's loyal community and live,
or chase after phantoms of evil and die.
PROVERBS 11:19 MSG

The better you get to know God, the more you'll understand how God wants you to respond to evil. And make no mistake, this world is inhabited by quite a few people very determined to do evil things. The devil and his human helpers are working 24/7 to cause pain and heartbreak in every corner of the globe . . . including your corner. So you'd better beware.

Your job, if you choose to accept it, is to recognize evil and fight it. The moment that you decide to fight evil whenever you see it, you can no longer be a lukewarm, halfhearted Christian. And, when you are no longer a lukewarm Christian, God rejoices while the devil despairs.

When will you choose to get serious about fighting the evils of our world? Before you answer that question, consider this: in the battle of good versus evil, the devil never takes a day off . . . and neither should you.

more stuff to think about

Indifference to evil is more insidious than evil itself;
it is more universal, more contagious, and more dangerous.

ABRAHAM J. HESCHEL

God loves you, and He yearns for you to turn away from
the path of evil. You need His forgiveness, and you need
Him to come into your life and remake you from within.

BILLY GRAHAM

He who passively accepts evil is as much involved in it as
he who helps to perpetrate it. He who accepts evil without
protesting against it is really cooperating with it.

MARTIN LUTHER KING, JR.

The Big Idea

There is darkness in this world, but God's light can
overpower any darkness.

Getting to Know Him

*Those who worship false gods turn their backs on all
God's mercies. But I will offer sacrifices to you with
songs of praise, and I will fulfill all my vows.
For my salvation comes from the LORD alone.*

JONAH 2:8-9 NLT

How much time do you spend getting to know God? A lot? A little? Almost none? The answer to this question will determine, to a surprising extent, the state of your spiritual health. And make no mistake: the more time and energy you invest with God, the better you'll come to know Him.

Are you making time each day to praise God and to study His Word? If so, you know firsthand the blessings that He offers those who worship Him consistently and sincerely. But, if you have unintentionally allowed the hustle and bustle of your busy day to come between you and your Creator, then you must slow down, take a deep breath, and rearrange your priorities. Now.

2 minutes A DAY

more stuff to think about

You're busy with all the pressures of the world around you, but in that busyness you're missing the most important element of all—God's ongoing presence that is available to you.

BILL HYBELS

This is a day when we are so busy doing everything that we have no time to be anything. Even religiously we are so occupied with activities that we have no time to know God.

VANCE HAVNER

There is an enormous power in little things to distract our attention from God.

OSWALD CHAMBERS

The Big Idea

If you're here, God is here. If you're there, God is, too. You can't get away from Him or His love . . . thank goodness!

Celebrate Life

This is the day which the LORD has made;
let us rejoice and be glad in it.
PSALM 118:24 NASB

Want to know God a little better? Try this: celebrate the life He has given you.

Do you feel like celebrating today? If you're a believer, you should! When you allow Christ to reign over your heart, today and every day should be a time for joyful celebration.

What do you expect from the day ahead? Are you expecting God to do wonderful things, or are you living beneath a cloud of worry and doubt? The words of Psalm 118:24 remind us that every day is a gift from God. So whatever this day holds for you, begin it and end it with God as your partner and Christ as your Savior. And throughout the day, give thanks to the One who created you and saved you. God's love for you is infinite. Accept it; celebrate it; and be thankful.

Some of us seem so anxious about avoiding hell that
we forget to celebrate our journey toward heaven.

PHILIP YANCEY

Celebration is possible only through the deep realization
that life and death are never found completely separate.
Celebration can really come about only where fear and love,
joy and sorrow, tear and smiles can exist together.

HENRI NOUWEN

The wonder of our Lord is that He is so accessible to us in
the common things of our lives: the cup of water . . .
breaking of the bread . . . welcoming children into
our arms . . . fellowship over a meal . . . giving thanks.
A simple attitude of caring, listening,
and lovingly telling the truth.

NANCIE CARMICHAEL

The Big Idea

If you don't feel like celebrating, start counting your
blessings. Before long, you'll realize that you have plenty of
reasons to celebrate.

GOD

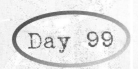

Open Up Your Heart

And we know that in all things God works for the good of those who love him, who have been called according to his purpose.

ROMANS 8:28 NIV

If you want to know God in a more meaningful way, you'll need to open up your heart and let Him in.

C. S. Lewis observed, "A person's spiritual health is exactly proportional to his love for God." If you hope to receive a full measure of God's spiritual blessings, you must invite your Creator to rule over your heart. When you honor God in this way, His love expands to fill your heart and bless your life.

St. Augustine wrote, "I love you, Lord, not doubtingly, but with absolute certainty. Your Word beat upon my heart until I fell in love with you, and now the universe and everything in it tells me to love you."

Today, open your heart to the Father. And let your obedience be a fitting response to His never-ending love.

2 minutes A DAY

more stuff to think about

If you want to know the will and voice of God, you must give the time and effort to cultivate a love relationship with Him. That is what He wants!

HENRY BLACKABY

Man was created by God to know and love Him in a permanent, personal relationship.

ANNE GRAHAM LOTZ

The truth of the Gospel is intended to free us to love God and others with our whole heart.

JOHN ELDREDGE

The Big Idea

Express Yourself: If you sincerely love God, don't be too bashful to tell Him so. And while you're at it, don't be too bashful to tell other people about your feelings. If you love God, say so!

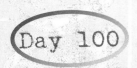

For God So Loved the World

*This is how much God loved the world: He gave his Son,
his one and only Son. And this is why:
so that no one need be destroyed; by believing in him
anyone can have a whole and lasting life.*

JOHN 3:16 MSG

For believers, death is not an ending; it is a beginning;
for believers, the grave is not a final resting-place, it is
a place of transition. For believers, death is not a dark
journey into nothingness; it is a homecoming.

God sent His Son as a sacrifice for our sins. Through
Jesus, we are redeemed. By welcoming Christ into our
hearts, we have received the precious, unfathomable gift of
eternal life. Let us praise God for His Son. The One from
Galilee has saved us from our sins so that we might live
courageously, die triumphantly, and live again—eternally.

2 minutes A DAY

more stuff to think about

Considering how I prepare for my children when
I know they are coming home, I love to think of the
preparations God is making for my homecoming one day.
He knows the colors I love, the scenery I enjoy, the things
that make me happy, all the personal details.

ANNE GRAHAM LOTZ

Man may dismiss compassion from his heart,
but God will never.

WILLIAM COWPER

Let us throw ourselves into the ocean of His goodness,
where every failing will be cancelled and anxiety
will be turned into love.

ST. PAUL OF THE CROSS

The Big Idea

Jesus loves you . . . His love is amazing, it's wonderful, and
it's meant for you.